Chasing Dreams

The True Story of the
Youngest Female Tevis Cup Champion

Sanoma Blakeley

SANTA
MONICA
PRESS

SANTA
MONICA
PRESS

Published by:
Santa Monica Press LLC
P.O. Box 850
Solana Beach, CA 92075
1-800-784-9553
www.santamonicapress.com
books@santamonicapress.com

Printed in China

Santa Monica Press books are available at special quantity discounts when purchased in bulk by corporations, organizations, or groups. Please call our Special Sales department at 1-800-784-9553.

ISBN-13 978-1-59580-123-4
Ebook ISBN: 978-1-59580-768-7

Library of Congress Cataloging-in-Publication Data

Publisher's Cataloging-in-Publication data

Names: Blakeley, Sanoma, author.
Title: Chasing dreams : the true story of the youngest female Tevis Cup champion / by Sanoma Blakeley.
Description: Solana Beach, CA: Santa Monica Press, 2023.
Identifiers: ISBN: 978-1-59580-123-4 (print) | 978-1-59580-768-7 (ebook)
Subjects: LCSH Blakeley, Sanoma. | Tevis Cup Ride. | Endurance riding (Horsemanship)--West (U.S.) | Horsemen and horsewomen--West (U.S.)--Biography. | Trails--West (U.S.) | BISAC BIOGRAPHY & AUTOBIOGRAPHY / Sports | SPORTS & RECREATION / Animal Sports / Equestrian | SPORTS & RECREATION / Animal Sports / Horse Racing | NATURE / Animals / Horses
Classification: LCC SF296.E5 B53 2023 | DDC 798.2/4--dc23

Cover and interior design and production by Future Studio
Cover photo of Sanoma Blakeley on Cougar Rock by Lisa Chadwick of Gore/Baylor Photography.
Back flap photo by David Brownell

Dedication

So many people and horses have come through my life and helped me evolve into who I am today, whether for a brief interaction or a lifelong relationship. I dedicate this book to everyone who helped me reach my goals and shape my life, and especially to my parents, Wasch and Gabriela, my brother, Barrak, and my favorite horses: Midnite, Focus, and Goober.

Contents

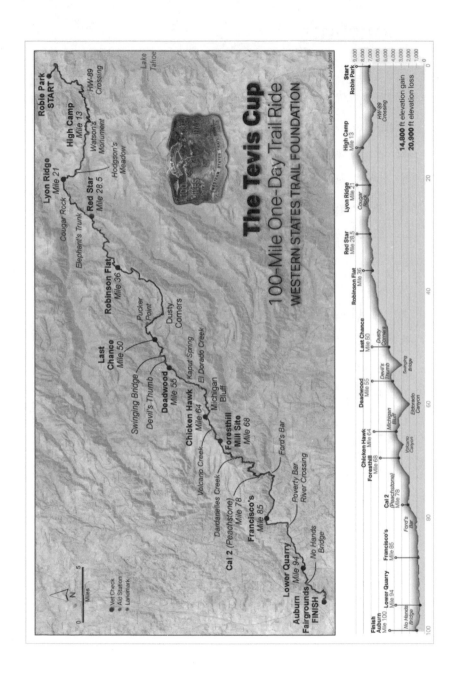

Tevis Cup trail map and elevation chart.

Introduction

In May of 1953, Edmund Hillary and Sherpa Tenzing Norgay were the first men to reach Mount Everest's summit and change the future of mountaineering. These daring men and their companions were the pioneers who, with endurance and determination, conquered the ultimate challenge in the sport they loved.

Two years after the first successful summit of Everest, Wendell Robie and a few of his friends found their own Everest: the Tevis Cup. They saddled up to prove that horses in the 1950s were just as tough as the horses that had carried gold across the Sierra Nevada Mountains in the 1800s, following the same route established by the miners across the mountains of Placer County and Gold Country, California. To win the bet, they would have to complete the whole 100-mile trek, from Truckee to Auburn, in under 24 hours. These men changed the future of the sport they loved: endurance horse racing.

After Mr. Robie successfully completed the 100-mile journey through some of the most rugged and treacherous mountains in North America, he established an annual endurance competition. Since then, horse-and-rider teams have raced across the Western States trail every year. The Western States Trail Ride quickly grew in popularity and soon adopted the nickname Tevis, after the trophy for the winning horse-and-rider team. The Tevis Cup was named for Lloyd Tevis (1824–1899) by his grandson, Will, a prominent San Francisco businessman and early benefactor of the ride. The shortest amount of time it took to complete the traditional 100-mile course was 10:46, by Boyd Zontelli riding Rushcreek Hans in 1981.

The Tevis Cup is the oldest and most famous modern-day endurance ride, and is limited to 250 participants each year. It is arguably the most challenging endurance horse race in the world, and successful riders flock from countries around the globe to compete. The race still holds the tradition of a 24-hour cut-off time, and requires riders to be over the age of 12 to enter. Gail Gilmer, the youngest rider to complete Tevis, was 11 years old in 1964; her actual age wasn't revealed until after the race. That same year, Neil Hutton became the youngest rider to win the Tevis Cup. He was only 17 years old.

The vast majority of the trail is only accessible by foot, horseback, or helicopter. There is 36,000 feet of elevation change, and the narrow, technical mountain trails are nothing to be toyed with. Often the hills are too steep to support a trail, so the trail is etched into the hillside in the form of switchbacks. There are a few sections where the switchbacks are so tight, your stirrup brushes the hillside.

Cougar Rock and Pucker Point are two of the most famous highlights of the 100-mile trail. A large volcanic rock outcropping, Cougar Rock can drain the blood from your extremities when you face it in person, knowing that your horse must scale it. Thousands of horses have successfully climbed this icon of the trail, and confidence is the key to conquering it. Photographers are eagerly waiting there to capture the looks of determination and partnership as horse-and-rider teams cross the intimidating rock mass.

Pucker Point lives up to its name. It is a thousand-foot sheer drop-off to the American River below, and the narrow bend in the trail passes only a few feet from the drop-off point. The scene of the canyons and Sierra Nevada Mountains will not only stop your heart, but also steal your breath. The views are worth the ride, but if you have a fear of heights, the trail balancing on the rocky cliffs overlooking the American River will wrench your gut.

From miles 50 to 68 of the race, the trail leads horse-and-rider teams through three precipitous canyons. The trail itself is enough of a challenge, but to add to it, the California heat consistently reaches triple digits. Rivers or creeks rush through each of the canyons, and the first canyon river is crossed by a swinging suspension bridge.

To complete the 100-mile journey through the mountains, riders begin the race under the full moon, riding through all hours of the daylight and finish the trail in the darkness again. At certain points of the race—for example, when the sun has set but the moon has yet to rise—the darkness is so dense, you can't see your horse's ears.

Besides navigating the rugged mountains, riders also ford the American River. The morning before the race, the dam up-river from the crossing point increases the amount of water held back so that the horses can safely cross. Even with the extra water suppressed, the river still reaches up your horse's sides, and you can feel your mount fighting the current of the swift river.

Veterinarians inspect the horses throughout the competition, and any horse showing signs of lameness or compromised health is pulled from the race. Rider fatigue, saddle rubs, heat stroke, and motion sickness can also stop riders from reaching the finish line. On average, only 50 percent of riders who start the Tevis Cup complete it.

As George S. Patton said, "They accept the challenges so that they can feel the exhilaration of victory."

CHAPTER 1

An Introduction to Endurance

What the heck am I doing? Well . . . it's now or never. These thoughts raced through my mind to the rhythm of my horse's hoofbeats as we galloped along the winding banks of the American River. The long, wearing day in the saddle had brought exhaustion, both physical and mental. But now was not the time for self-doubt.

Only 11 miles to go. If everything goes to plan, we will be done in an hour and a half. Under normal circumstances, making it through these last 11 miles through California's Gold Country would be a challenging feat in itself. But, compared to the 89 miles we had already conquered, I didn't even bat an eye at the winding inclines leading to the Auburn fairgrounds.

I inhaled sharply, clearing my mind of negative thoughts and replacing them with the ultimate determination with which I had started the race. *If the Reynolds' horses can do it, so can yours. You can't win if you don't fight for it. You didn't train your whole life to back down now.*

The golden sun melted into the horizon, summoning the light of the day to accompany it. It was still light enough to illuminate the American River, fed from snowmelt high in the Sierras. Barely visible was the single-lane dirt road, about the width of a car, that the race followed. It was that time in the evening when my eyes could still see the road, but my depth perception was failing. Groves of scrub oak peppered with eucalyptus lined the trail. Dry and brittle grass that hadn't seen moisture since the spring rains welcomed the descending coolness of night-time. Beside the green riverbanks, the heat from the summer had taken its toll on the landscape. The dust from the Western States Trail that I had tasted for the better part of the day clung to my sweat-covered face like a mask.

I was in the perfect position to shoot for the win. But things could change so fast, and I didn't want to count on anything. With 89 miles down, I was speeding along more quickly than I had ever gone that late in a race, on trails I did not know. My horse Goober and I charged into uncharted territory, tucked behind the two leading horse-and-rider teams, Jeremy and Heather Reynolds—the United States' best endurance racers. Between the two of them, they had won the Tevis Cup seven times. This couple had ridden worldwide, representing the U.S. team at the World Equestrian Games, and here I was, 18 years old, racing alongside them.

Darkness was approaching, and the race was far from over. Even if it didn't end in victory, it would still be the race of my life.

Riding came naturally to me. My brother and I inherited our love of horses from my parents, who have both shared a passion for horses since they were kids.

My dad grew up exploring the Oregon outback on horse-back, herding sheep with his brothers on the family ranch. He related childhood stories of working hard all summer to save up to buy his first horse, Whiskey Jim. I was fascinated by the stories of him swinging up on Whiskey Jim by his mane and galloping all over the desert bareback, jumping logs and reading books with his horse. My older brother, Barrak, and I wanted to be just as adventurous as our Pa, but with the style of our mom.

Mom's family couldn't afford a horse, but this didn't stifle her love for them. Growing up in Essen, Germany, she would spend her allowance on riding lessons and trade cleaning stalls for time in the saddle.

Traveling was the center of my mother's life in her early twenties. While some people go to college, my mom struck out to see the world, only coming home to earn enough money to head out again. She backpacked throughout South America and Central America, eventually ending up in North America. The last stop on her journey before heading back to Germany was a small island in Alaska. In the tiny fishing community of Ketchikan, she met an outgoing blonde woman named Pilar, who helped my mom get a part-time job and offered her accommodation.

The two girlfriends were stopped at a traffic light, my mom in the passenger seat, when a handsome young man pulled up next to the car on his bike, recognizing it was his sister's. He leaned against the open window of the car to talk to his sister. His uniquely green eyes made contact with Mom's dark-brown eyes. *Someday, that woman is going to be my wife,* Wasch thought.

That short exchange of introductions led them through romance's door. After only getting to know my mother for a few days, the romantic young man scaled a cliff to spray-paint "Gabriela" onto the rocks. It was the first sign of many to show his true feelings.

After earning enough money for a plane ticket home, my mother headed for the airport. But her admirer wouldn't let her get away that easily. Shortly after she left, Wasch arrived in Germany and courted the beautiful brunette by climbing the gutters to her fourth-story bedroom window to deliver love letters. He also met my somewhat intimidating grandparents, who didn't speak a word of English. My grandfather was a stern German man who had lost both his legs in World War II. My grandmother had fled Berlin on one of the Allied tanks when she was still a teenager. Grandpa's intense gaze challenged this Alaskan timber faller, guarding his prized daughter. He would be a hard man for Wasch to impress.

Wasting no time, within two weeks of their first encounter, my dad was on one knee proposing marriage to my mother.

"What?" Mom said. "No! I barely know you. Give me more time."

A few days later, they had the same conversation.

And again, not long after that.

My dad, not giving up, quickly asked again for the fourth time.

"Stop asking me," Mom told him. "I like you, but I'm not ready to get married."

Dejected, my father knew that if he left now, he might never see Gabriela again.

It was the happiest day of my grandmother's life watching the American boy walk out into the rain, bound for the airport. Wasch tried to hitchhike, but nobody wanted him in their car; he was soaking wet and looked miserable with his broken heart. So, he took the underground metro to the central train station, planning to take the train to the airport and fly to warm Africa to clear his head and mend his heart.

As he waited to board the train, my dad thought it was a mirage when he saw my mother running up the platform toward him.

"What made you come?" he asked as they held each other on the platform.

"I knew if I let you go now, I would be saying goodbye forever," Mom replied. "I couldn't do that. Yes, I will marry you."

They spent most of their first years as a couple commuting between Alaska and Germany. Then they moved to Oregon and built the log home where they would raise their children. When the house was almost completed, Pa surprised my mom with a little quarter-horse mare named Candy, a gift that fulfilled Mom's childhood dreams of owning her own horse. There is hardly a more significant commitment to a home than having a horse in a corral.

Since my parents like to do things together, they bought a second horse for my dad, an ex-endurance mare out of the "Nickel Ad" for $500. She had been a successful racehorse before being retired for a tendon injury. Several years of pasture turnout had healed her injury, and we called her Try-Again and gave her a second chance.

My parents enjoyed their time in the saddle, which allowed for a brief distraction from their two very young kids. I grew up riding horses, and it was like learning a second language that I'd always known. Pictures in my childhood photo albums show me on top of Candy, my legs too short to reach even halfway down the saddle flaps.

As they got more into the local riding scene, they discovered a connection to Dolly Decair, an older, fiery woman who had moved up to Oregon from California. She quickly became a close family friend, and I considered her to be my third grandma.

Dolly and I shared a love of horses and, despite hardly being old enough to understand the extent of her success as an endurance racer, I was captivated by the tales she told of racing with her stallion. She inspired both me and my parents. Racing a horse, not only against other riders but against the elements and physical limits, made the sport of endurance racing a true challenge.

Photos hung on Dolly's walls of her and her horse conquering the famous Cougar Rock, a volcanic mass that is a symbol of the most challenging 100-mile endurance race: the Tevis Cup. Listening to her stories of competing in the Tevis Cup left me with chills. Dolly shared memories of galloping up the rugged canyons and racing alongside some of the best endurance racers in history. I vividly remember the story she told about letting go of winning the Tevis six miles from the finish, opting to let her horse refuel and spend more time eating, and coming in 2nd with a fresher, healthier horse. I admired that, despite her competitive desires, she always chose her horse's well-being over winning.

It was the thrilling stories Dolly told us about the Tevis Cup that inspired my family to try the sport. My parents were determined to start training. The race was exceptionally demanding—summer heat, grueling climbs, narrow paths, thousands of feet of elevation change, endless canyons, riding in the dark, the 24-hour cut-off time, and crossing multiple rivers, including the American River. The Tevis Cup was the ultimate challenge of endurance racing.

This was the sport my dad's Arabian was bred for and had previously succeeded in. Though Candy could go for hours, she preferred the short sprint across the pasture. Scanning the newspaper classifieds, my parents looked for a second Arabian to match Pa's horse and compete in endurance races. They came across an ad for an Arabian gelding, Victor, who happened to be about 15 minutes from our home.

Driving home in their old Toyota Land Cruiser with my brother and I in the backseat, my parents were infatuated with this horse. Victor was the son of a racing stallion that had set track records. Sherode Powers, the man who owned Victor, also shared his advice on endurance racing with my parents, who knew practically nothing about the sport at the time.

Victor was the first horse to give my parents a sleepless night of deciding whether or not to purchase. He was over their budget, but was also the most amazing animal they had ever had the option to own. The next morning, they picked up Victor in their red two-horse trailer, inspired to try out the sport of endurance horse racing.

My parents had found a sport that all four of us could take on together, as a family. They taught my brother and I to ride at a very young age. My memories of Mom teaching me to balance on a horse are vague but remain etched in my consciousness.

"Do the flying eagle," she would instruct me. She taught me how to put my arms out to my sides, parallel to the ground, showing me how to balance without my hands on the reins.

"Now, close your eyes." I rode Victor, who was an excellent babysitter with kids but a go-getter when my mom was on him. With my arms out and eyes closed, it felt like the closest thing to flying. On the tall gelding, my feet barely reached the stirrups on the shortest setting, but I didn't need a saddle to feel free from the earth below me. I pictured my horse galloping on the beach, his hoofbeats echoing against the firm, wet sand. In my imagination, the sound of the crashing waves and cawing seagulls accompanied the salty air that coyly kissed my cheeks. With my eyes closed, I felt freedom, like an eagle soaring through the air.

But I would soon snap back to reality. I couldn't hold my eyes shut very long or I would start teetering, losing the rhythm of Victor's significant strides.

At about five years old, I had my first and only riding lesson with a well-known dressage instructor. My parents were working on improving their form, and they were picking up some tips from this expert. After they finished, I had a brief lesson of my own. We hoped to get a few exercises that my parents could work on with me to improve my riding.

"Can I gallop?" I wanted to show off for the instructor. A few days before, I had galloped Victor for the first time. Only a few short strides, but until that point it was my proudest moment in riding.

A look of terror filled her face at the thought of me galloping. "How about not?" she said with a grimace as she watched me try to keep my balance with Victor's massive stride. I looked like a ragdoll crossed with a bobblehead, bouncing atop the saddle with my Megamind helmet.

After a very brief lesson, the dressage instructor had some frank words with my parents. They remember it word for word.

"Your daughter looks like a monkey riding a dog," she told them. "Have you considered getting her a pony? I think it would be a much better match."

Instead of a pony, my seven-year-old brother Barrak got a rather stubborn Arabian gelding that we shared. Flusi was the perfect kid's horse when we went to buy him. Once we brought him home, though, we were pretty sure he had been sedated before we looked at him because, suddenly, he was way more spirited. The gelding was quite the character and tested me and my brother often by cutting through the sagebrush without warning.

Flusi taught us a lot about riding. We might not have had the perfect posture or ridden "properly," but we could hang on and stick with a horse. Maybe I did look like a monkey riding a sassy Arab, but that didn't stop me from doing what I loved.

Kindergarten only took up half of my mornings during the week. About once a week, during the other half of the day, my parents would take me riding on the trails near our home. I loved that special time I had alone with my parents while my big brother was in school. I rode Victor on our after-school rides, and my dad rode his spicy little fireball. From the top of his horse, Pa would "pony" Victor, which meant holding on to the leadline that gave him partial control of Victor. If anything happened to the horse I was riding or to me, he was always only a rope's length away. I felt safe riding this way, and it gave me confidence on the trail.

As it happened, Victor wiggled to the right side of my dad, but the lead rope was still in his left hand. The result was that the rope slid right under Pa's horse's tail, creating a wedgie for horses. His horse took off bucking, and my dad, taken by surprise, fell off.

"What are you doing down there?" I asked at the odd sight of my dad on the ground.

By the end of my kindergarten year, I was able to take off the "training wheels" and ride Victor without the extra guidance from my dad.

In 2004, my family showed up to my parents' first endurance race. My dad would be riding his mare, and my mom had brought Victor along. We were singing on the drive to the race, and my parents were so excited to finally compete.

A few hours later, we were no longer singing, but driving home feeling dejected. The vet had told my parents that their horses weren't ready for the race and hadn't let them start.

My parents learned from that experience and did what it took to train and get their two horses ready for the next race a few months later. At this one, they had a blast racing and placed fairly well. My grandpa came along and watched me and my brother while my parents were racing. Barrak and I were in heaven, looking at all the pretty horses and cheering like the couple of crazy kids that we were when my parents crossed the finish line.

My mom and dad didn't realize how much strain it is on the body to ride a horse for 30 miles. They could hardly walk down the stairs the next morning, they were so sore from spending over three hours trotting the previous day. They hadn't even done an actual endurance race yet, since the course must be 50 miles or over in length to be considered an endurance race. Races under that mileage are categorized as a "limited distance" race.

After that first race, my parents moved up to 50-mile races. The more they learned about the sport, the more intrigued they were, with the ultimate goal of someday making it to the Tevis Cup.

Three years into their endurance careers, my parents competed in the Tevis Cup for the first time. I was only six and can't recall much about that first trip to Tevis. The day before the race, I'd consumed an unhealthy amount of the electrolytes meant for our horses.

Before and during races, riders administer minerals to their horses to help prevent any deficiencies during the competition. Minerals like sodium, potassium, and magnesium are unpleasant for the horses to consume, so riders mix the electrolytes with applesauce, molasses, and other more palatable substances for better absorption and so it doesn't taste so bad for the horses. The particular electrolytes I ate were mixed with dextrose, giving them a sweet taste that was very appealing to me. I was like a bear in a beehive, scooping sugary minerals into my mouth.

My memories were of fever, headaches, and my parents' race crew forcing me to drink a lot of water. My molars were also erupting, which was the main cause of my sickness. Between those uncomfortable moments, I remember waiting at the finish line, watching the first horses come in, and gaping at the top 10 competitors. I was blown away by the winning horse and its rider, Jeremy Reynolds. Jeremy's confidence and professionalism left an impression on me. He seemed to be doing the impossible, winning Tevis for the second time.

Jeremy's horse looked proud and accomplished, having tackled the challenging trail and crossed the finish line like a god. I'll never forget the sparkle in the horse's eyes and how it seemed to carry its head just a bit higher. The level of fitness that the equine athlete possessed and the unison of Reynolds' crew working together to assist the competitors during the race was beautiful to watch.

The next morning, the top 10 finishers gathered in McCain Stadium to present their horses to the vets for the Haggin Cup judging. This is an award given to the horse finishing in the most superior condition. The contrast between the novices and these experienced riders presenting their horses for the Haggin Cup was astounding. My mom finished her very first 100-mile race at 2:56 in the morning, about five and a half hours behind the winner. We were so proud of Victor coming in 27th place out of 183 starters and 95 finishers. Mom was tired, sore, and chafed.

My dad did not finish; Try-Again had a muscle tie-up, and their race was cut short at 28 miles. She was still getting fluids administered intravenously in the treatment barn. The race had chewed them up and spit them out. They were humbled, to say the least. We weren't even close to being able to compete alongside these top riders and their well-conditioned horses, but the awe and inspiration stuck, and someday I knew I was going to compete in Tevis, too. One day I would be in that stadium, showing off my horse to some of the country's best veterinarians, and one day I would be handed the microphone to give a winning speech at the award ceremony.

CHAPTER 2

My First Race

In my opinion, endurance is the purest equine sport. The countless hours in the saddle require a true bond with your horse, and you have to be able to connect and almost become one with your horse in order to win. The first horse and rider to cross the finish line and pass the final veterinarian examination is the winning team, plain and simple. Buying the best gear or a proven horse will only take you so far. The amount of work and sweat you put in as a team determines how successful you will be.

Even if the sport of endurance racing is not as well-known in the horse community, just about every country has an endurance organization. The American Endurance Ride Conference is the main organization that sanctions endurance races in the United States. Their motto is: *To finish is to win.* Having that motto promotes a great sport, in which families and couples often compete together as a team.

At the lower levels of the sport and at the local races, almost everybody is very friendly and helpful. It was the perfect sport to grow up in, as it is family-oriented and supports the next generation of riders. Since the AERC doesn't allow prize money, the competition is a lot less cutthroat than in other disciplines or organizations. At smaller, local rides, there are hardly any spectators, as the horses and riders are out on the trail for several hours at a time and there is not much to see. If someone shows up to a race without a horse to ride, they will often be put to work to crew for the rider they came to support.

Endurance racing often feels more like a community than a competition. The lack of spectators results in a lack of sponsors, and when there is no money in a sport, it remains a hobby. In the United States it is not a very popular sport and even in the horse world, not everybody has heard of endurance racing. The fact that it is not an Olympic sport makes it even more obscure. There are some races, though, like the National Championships and the Tevis Cup, that are increasingly well-known and competitive.

Being in good physical shape as a rider is vital to riding a horse for 50 to 100 miles, and as long as the horses are in good condition, any age of human can compete.

The more you are willing to learn and adapt, the further you will go, because there is always room for improvement. Not only is there competition between competitors, but 50 or 100 miles of grueling trail gets to you just as much. Simple accidents, like a rock on the trail or your horse having a bad day, can end your race early.

While it is fun to race and let your horse run like a bat out of hell, much more is involved. At the end of the day, the important thing is not if you won the race, but that your horse is healthy and uninjured. That is what mandatory holds at checkpoints throughout the race are for. Your race time is paused and a veterinarian examines your horse. There is a list of things the vets check for, and if your horse does not meet any one of the requirements to continue, they can pull you out of the race. There are many reasons for being pulled, but the most common are rider option, metabolic, or lameness issues.

At the vet check, the veterinarians measure your horse's heart rate to ensure that it is recovering properly and not too tired to continue. They also measure the gut-sounds to make sure the horses are eating, and check for signs of dehydration. Riders have to trot the horses out for the vets, who are searching for any subtle signs of lameness or fatigue. It is heartbreaking to be pulled from a race, but the high standards for competing ensure that excellent care is given to the horses and makes it extra satisfying to finish.

When I was seven, I got my first horse that I didn't have to share with Barrak or my mom. Midnite was the best horse I could have asked for. We were both seven years old when our timelines intertwined. We depended on each other, and I was just as important to Midnite as she was to me.

My parents had bought Midnite for a very low price and were training her. In her sales ad, the previous owner had written: "NOT A KID'S HORSE." Indeed, Midnite was extremely stubborn and had a strong mind of her own. My parents determined that her behavior issues stemmed from her anxiety and insecurity. However, as soon as they put me on her, she was a completely different horse. She melted like butter and was as soft and sweet as a horse could be.

For me and Barrak, our favorite playmates were our two horses. I had my Midnite, and he had his Boogsy, and we did just about everything with them. On the weekends, we would wake up early, dress up like cowboys, and sneak out the window in the guest bedroom so the front door would remain locked and our parents would think we were asleep.

In our second-hand cowboy hats and boots, we would practice mounting our horses like Pa used to do when he was a kid, swinging up bareback from their manes. We learned other ways to get on them unconventionally—leapfrogging from behind, or even getting their heads down, laying across their necks, and hoisting ourselves onto their backs. With my brother and me on their backs, we came up with all sorts of crazy ways to ride them, sitting side saddle or backwards. Then we would stand on our two patient steads and dismount by sliding off their butts.

Sitting on our horses bareback and letting them wander around their pen without any tack, we carried around an old rawhide lass rope just to complete our cowboy costumes. We tried throwing the rope off the horses a few times, but my rope-throwing skills were hopeless and I quickly gave up.

Barrak and I dreamed of living on the range. We would sit in our forts after riding bareback all afternoon and make plans of how we would buy a big ranch and cut our own hair. I was Barrak's little shadow. Whenever he had an idea, I wanted to do it, too. He loved his Boogsy and was always suggesting fun things we could do with our horses besides just riding down the trail.

On lazy summer days, we would occasionally try our hand at jousting with PVC pipes. Barrak and I set up jousting lanes in the horses' paddock, so they had to run past each other without veering to the side. Unfortunately, Boogsy was the dominant horse, and when Midnite and I got too close, he would put his ears back and chase her away. When it got too hot outside, we would take our two trusty steeds to the neighbor's pond and swim with them. Poor Midnite and Boogsy had to put up with everything: jumping, swimming, jousting, and playing cowboy.

That same year, at seven years old, I competed in my first 25-mile race. I proudly brought my ribbon to school the next day for show and tell. I owned the title of "The Horse-Crazy Girl" in my class. Throughout school, whenever anyone said the word "horse," I was the girl all heads turned to. Going to school in a small community, I knew my classmates well; it was the same 30 kids from kindergarten through eighth grade. I was always a little distant from my classmates, and although I got along well with everyone, my best friends were Barrak and my horse, Midnite.

Several months after completing that 25-mile race, Midnite and I were training for our first 50-miler. The race we picked would be in Nevada in April 2009. To get Midnite and myself ready for the race, my parents would often pick up my brother and I from school with the horse trailer, and we would head straight to the Henderson Flats trailhead to condition our horses. Henderson Flats became my second home. From the trailhead, there are endless miles of trails for hill work, flat work, and speedwork. In preparation for the early spring race, we trained during the winter. I would often finish the last few miles of our ride in the dark when the days were short.

On one of those after-school rides, we had planned to train to the top of Gray Butte, which is about 5,100 feet in elevation. Riding to the top gave us a solid 2,000-foot climb from the Henderson Flats trailhead. My parents planned that ride in correspondence to a full moon, since the 15-mile ride would take several hours and we would not be able to get it done in the limited daylight.

A few days before our planned ride to Gray Butte, we received a heavy snowfall. We didn't let the snow or darkness stop us from getting ready for my first 50-mile race, so we put on our snow boots, saddled up, and hit the trail.

There is hardly a more magical experience than breaking a fresh trail through the snow on a horse. We had a fun first part of the ride, but once we reached the top of Gray Butte it was completely dark. We dismounted our horses to walk them down by hand, since downhills put a lot of strain on horses' legs.

I couldn't feel my toes. They were completely frozen and numb. Walking down in the dark and snow, I was sobbing, doubting this was all worth the effort. My parents let Midnite follow their horses, and Mom carried my boots while Pa put me on his shoulders and tucked my popsicle feet into the sleeves of his sweater. As we walked a bit over a mile down Gray Butte, my feet slowly thawed and the full moon popped out of the horizon. It was so big and close, I felt like I could reach out and grab it from the top of my dad's shoulders.

I have hardly ever felt more connected to the world and to reality as being out riding at night, the full moon shining over everything.

By the time we reached the bottom of Gray Butte and re-mounted, my toes were toasty warm. The full moon reflected on the perfectly white snow, and I forgot all about the misery of being cold and was completely content right there with my horse and my family. As we descended out of the hills and closer to the trailer, I looked behind me and caught my breath as the full moon silhouetted the hills and cast our shadows over the snow. This was what it would be like to race Tevis someday. Riding under the full moon, in complete unison with my horse.

As the days got longer, so did our rides. We were regularly doing rides between 20 and 30 miles to prepare for the Nevada Derby, and by the time April rolled around, I felt about as prepared as I could be.

Besides training for the race, I also wanted my beautiful mare Midnite to stand out in the crowd of horses at our first 50-mile race. To do this, I polished her hoofs with bright-green nail polish and braided her mane and tail.

The ride camp was located in a sea of sagebrush, and there

were no trees to slow the howling wind. The barbed-wire fence that surrounded the ride camp was lined with tumbleweeds that had blown across the desert and created a natural wall. As the wind came off the mountains and whipped its way around the trailers and horses, we set up blankets to block the wind for the horses. It dried out my skin and filled my eyes with sand.

Once we started the race, the April wind gusts just about blew tiny me out of the saddle as we crossed the high desert and got into the Nevada high country. There was snow on the side of the trail, and the north hillsides were still frozen. The freezing temperatures made for a real endurance experience. I have never in my life wanted to quit as badly as I did during that first 50-mile race.

About halfway through, I was flung off of Midnite. She had been grazing, as she always liked to do. We had a mutual agreement that she could do what she wanted as long as she took care of me. Suddenly, Midnite realized the other horses hadn't stopped to eat with her, and she took off at a dead run, slamming on the brakes when she caught up to them. This was nothing new to me, but this time the only trouble was she stopped on a very steep downhill, propelling me between her ears to the ground.

The first lesson my parents taught me in riding a horse is you *always* get back on. So, despite everything—my hurt pride and body aches from coming off Midnite unexpectedly—I got back on.

I finished in 6th place and was officially an endurance rider! Only four more years until I would be old enough to compete in Tevis.

Following my first 50-mile race, I lost my confidence from my unplanned dismount and didn't ride Midnite for the rest of the race season. Instead, I did a couple of races with Victor. But by the time winter rolled around, I had gained enough confidence to get back on Midnite and, despite my fears, try again.

Over the next several years, Midnite and I bonded again and she did everything for me. I would lay on her bareback, my bare feet on her butt with her fur between my toes, looking up at the sky while she ate grass. I would read Nancy Drew books either sitting at her feet while she ate, or on top of her.

Midnite gave everything for me. Not only was she my best babysitter, but she was also a competitive race horse. One of my favorite races with Midnite was in Idaho. Almost every year in October, I would take half a week off school and my family would make a vacation out of the Owyhee rides. Midnite won a couple of the races there, and I loved having my tent set up right by where she was munching on hay. She loved her job, and was always right with my parents' horses. No matter what I asked, she would do it, whether it was crossing rivers, going faster to race more experienced riders, or letting me bury my face in her mane to cry after a bad day at school.

Midnite taught me so much. There is no bond like the one with your first horse. She taught me to get back on, to keep going, to not to give up.

My family took the next few years to prepare better for the Tevis Cup. We learned a lot and when Barrak had finally reached the minimum age my family made the drive back to California. Our horses were stronger, and we had done our homework to avoid the same mistakes that had occurred on my parents' first Tevis attempt. Barrak got to ride with my mom, and I was able to enjoy crewing with Pa. I was happy to be able to spend time with Pa, but I was also jealous of Barrak; I wanted to take Midnite and ride Tevis, too. As a younger sister, I felt like those two years between us were to my disadvantage, since I had to watch Barrak doing cool things before I could.

In 2011, I could comprehend Tevis a lot better, now that I was in good health and a little older. The course had been rerouted and postponed because of the snow in the high-country.

My mom and Barrak were doing well, and seemed to have found a good rhythm. About 60 miles into the race, we were patiently waiting for them to arrive at the vet check when Pa pointed out a bay horse. The bay had an air of excellence. As he came into the vet check, he seemed very in tune with the race. He had a real head on his shoulders.

"I think that's the winning horse right there," Pa whispered to me. It wasn't until a few seconds later that we realized the horse, Riverwatch, belonged to Jeremy Reynolds.

At 68 miles, Pa and I were working hard crewing for Barrak and Mom. Victor was seasoned and breezed through the vet check. Hami, Mom's horse, always took a couple of minutes longer to pulse, so my dad and I were imitating Jeremy's crew and drenched him in cold water. Unfortunately, Hami wasn't used to that and the cold water shocked his hot muscles. His hind muscles turned rock hard and were locked up. He cramped so hard that it was almost dark by the time we were finally able to loosen his muscles. Hannah had generously offered to sponsor Barrak and he continued on without Mom as we continued massaging and stretching Hami.

After finally working Hami through his cramp and sending my mom down the trail, Pa and I zoomed back to the fairgrounds to watch the winning horse finish. Pa knows a good horse when he sees one, and sure enough, Jeremy and Riverwatch were the first to finish. It was Jeremy's third Tevis Cup win, and he seemed like a professional. Several hours later, Barrak and faithful Victor finished in 21st place.

Although Barrak and Victor did well, we still had a plethora to learn. Mom finished quite a while later in 73rd place.

Until that time, I didn't realize how much I wanted to do Tevis myself. The atmosphere at the finish and seeing my brother living our dream gave me the bug. But I didn't want to do it with just any horse; I wanted to ride a horse like Riverwatch, who had conquered the trail. The following morning at the Haggin Cup judging, the top 10 horses seemed levels ahead of our own. Riverwatch won that award as well. Watching the Reynoldses from afar was inspiring. We were just a family from Oregon and they didn't know who we were, but someday, I wanted to be racing alongside them at their level.

CHAPTER 3

Welcoming Goober Home

Growing up, money was always tight in my family. We loved racing endurance but couldn't afford expensive horses and equipment. So, we looked for the rejects, the horses people had discarded, given up on, or couldn't train, and we gave them jobs. Some of our best horses weren't pretty or focused enough for the show ring. Some of them bucked, were considered "dangerous," or their breeders were, for whatever reason, unable to care for their high-strung horses. We gave these horses a second chance, and many became outstanding endurance competitors.

To support our horse addiction, my parents bought these cheap, problematic horses, trained them, raced them, and then resold them to afford our personal horses. My family loved finding horses that had been given up on and giving them a chance. It became more than a business, as we were able to watch the transformation in these horses.

My mom regularly searched the local Craigslist for good deals, whether it was cheap lumber, furniture, or a horse. One late winter day in 2011, she stumbled across an ad for a free, nearly two-year-old Arabian gelding named Ares. We thought this free horse could be a fun challenge, and if he didn't work out for us, we could always sell him. My mom contacted the seller and asked for a bit of additional information.

The first question Mom posed was: Why is a well-bred

Arabian gelding being given away for free on Craigslist? The owner's reason for rehoming him was a move across the country. As to why he was free, it was a combination of the uncertainty of both the economy and his health.

My mom asked for a more detailed description of Ares's health. The owner, Allison, replied that she had noticed he seemed sore in his hind end while blasting around the pasture, and she'd brought him out of the field to investigate the cause. She made an appointment at Bend Equine Veterinary Clinic, one of the top vet clinics in central Oregon specializing in lameness. After extensive flexion tests and radiographs, Allison was devastated to hear that the horse was diagnosed with OCD (osteochondritis dissecans) in his stifles (a joint in a horse's hind legs similar to human knees).

The vet speculated that since Ares had grown so fast, his stifles had not developed properly. The vet put him on bone and joint supplements, but his career as a sport horse appeared to be over. This news was crushing to Allison, who had hoped to turn him into a performance horse. There was a slim chance that with time and supplements, he would outgrow it, but Allison could not afford to move him across the country if he had OCD that could flare up at any given moment.

My parents were intrigued and met with Allison and her young horse. Ares was born in Spokane, Washington, in April of 2009. He was well bred, with some famous horses in his lineage. As soon as Allison brought Ares into the arena and removed his halter to let him show off for my parents, my mom knew we would be bringing him home. Ares was happy to have an audience to show off for. With his tail curled high over his back and nostrils flared, he snorted around the arena. He lifted his black legs high and pranced around in the deep sand of the enclosure. Mom loved his spirit and his movement and vowed to always take good care of him.

We decided to give Ares a chance and welcomed him to our stable full of high-quality reject horses. They surrounded the gate when we got home, anxious to meet the new guy.

Ares's big brown eyes took in the new surroundings after being unloaded from our trailer. He went straight to exploring his new pen, walking along the sturdy log fence to inspect his new home's boundaries. It was a large, dry lot with many overgrown juniper trees. In the center of the corral was a large log barn. My parents had built it as a spec home, but they couldn't sell it when the economy crashed a few years earlier. The price of the logs was a fraction of what a traditional barn would have cost to build. After putting a roof on it and converting the kitchen area into stalls and the second story into hay storage, our unusual barn got many compliments.

"Your horse's barn is cooler than our house," visitors often joked as they got a look at the barn.

Converting the home into a barn, we blocked off a section where the bedroom would have been and made it a feeder. We filled that section with hay and let the horses free-choice eat through the windows from outside. In between the ground-level hay storage and the stalls is a wide hallway that would most likely have been the living room; now it lets the horses wander in and out of the barn as they please.

Whenever we got new horses that were used to living in a barn, they started out wanting to stay indoors, where they had access to the hay from inside the barn's common area. However, over time they got accustomed to being outside and gradually preferred to hang out under the trees rather than in the barn. Ares adjusted quickly, loving his freedom to move in and out of the barn as he pleased. He loved his new home and his new friends, forming a particular bond with a five-year-old gelding we had at the time. The two of them got into a lot of trouble together.

We were looking for a new name for Ares, as we had a mare named Heiress and didn't want to have two horses with a name pronounced the same way. At the time, my dad was learning a new song on the piano, and the piece was called "Finn McCool." We liked the title and tried to name our new horse Finn McCool, but this horse was anything but cool. He quickly earned the nickname Goober, for all the silly mischief he got into. As hard as we tried to rename him, Goober stuck.

This obnoxious two-year-old loved to bug the older, serious racehorses. Goober would provoke them and then be surprised when they bit him. He and his pal, Shai, were a fun pair to watch. They would bite onto each other's halters and lead each other around the corral. Goober had tremendous knot-untying skills. We would find the halters of other horses he'd set free scattered throughout the pen. Whenever we had a horse tied up, he would untie them.

He soon moved on to untying the gates, releasing the herd to run through our quiet neighborhood. Thankfully, we had very patient neighbors. We tried every way to tie the gate: chains and double knots. But the only thing that Goober couldn't open was a metal carabiner. We soon put carabiners on all the gates.

"How did this bucket end up in the barn?" someone would ask. "I thought it was by the gate."

"Ask Goober," was the inevitable reply.

As a youngster, Goober didn't show any soreness from his OCD and we were curious to see how he would turn out as an endurance horse. We had high hopes for him, but with his playful personality we wondered if he would have what it took to be a champion. We never could have imagined that, eight years later, he would become one of the top endurance horses in the country.

The back corner of our property had a sturdy round-pen built from hand-peeled logs my parents and grandpa had logged out of the forest south of Bend. Grandpa and his team of Percheron workhorses logged the pine forests; there are pictures of me, so small I could barely walk, sitting on top of these gentle giants with a log in tow, helping collect the timbers used to build our house and corral.

The round pen has welcomed a lot of horses over the years. Many horses wore a saddle for the first time within its borders. Its safety and security were felt by the horses, demonstrated by the consistent progress they made in their training there. The soothing gurgle of the nearby irrigation canal brought water and serenity to the horses from the nearby mountain's snow-melt. Our small property is an oasis in the desert, in contrast to central Oregon's sagebrush and dust-covered landscape.

Barrak and I rode the bus to and from school. It would let us out at the end of our road, about a mile from our house. We used to ride our bikes there, but after they got stolen, we had to run home. After a long day of brain exertion, we came home to lean against the round pen's smooth logs and watch my parents work with young, inexperienced horses. It was a beautiful thing to see the daily progress of an untrained horse.

Finally, it was Goober's turn to carry the saddle and have the bit in his mouth. Since he was still young when we began his saddle training, we didn't pressure him. Our objective wasn't to take him out for many rides, but to get him accustomed to it first. We wanted him to grow up knowing what his job was, so that being ridden would seem like a natural part of his life when he was older.

Goober got the hang of it pretty quickly, and after his first

few rides on the property, he was ready to see the trail. To condition the horses for longer rides and hill work, we had to load
them in the horse trailer and head to a trailhead, but we often
rode from the property for more casual daily training.

The ride through the neighborhood, navigating around gar-
bage cans and going past barking dogs and flags flapping in the
wind, wasn't even the most stressful part of riding from home.
Once we had made it through the neighborhood and emerged
out of the rosehip groves onto the backside of a rest area along
Highway 97, we were on public land. Then we had to cross an
unused highway bridge suspended over a 300-foot canyon. In
the summer, the bridge was a place where adrenaline junkies
flocked to bungee-jump.

Once across the bridge, we would come to a trail running
parallel to the railroad tracks. We rode confidently on that trail
with more solid horses, but I would rather have the bungee-jump
adrenaline rush than encounter a freight train with a young horse.

"Do you think Goober is ready to head out and go for a ride
through the park?" my dad asked my mom one day. Mom had
been the main one riding Goober.

"I guess I'm feeling a little suicidal today," my mom joked,
agreeing to the challenge of Goober's first off-property ride.

The chance of encountering a train was not a good option
with a young horse, so we played tag in a flat clearing a ways
off the tracks. Playing tag is a great way to train a horse to be
responsive and go where you want them to. The bonus, though,
is that it is a blast, whether you're running away or chasing.

Barrak and I were galloping through the sagebrush with
Boogsy and Midnite, riding bareback and trying to get our horses to jump the big bushes without plowing through them. We
were goofing off, hiding behind juniper trees, and tagging each
other, and we had forgotten my mom was on a young horse.

"Ahhh!" The scream came from where we had last seen Mom. Goober popped out from behind a tree, minus his rider.

"Are you okay?" we yelled to my mom. We were relieved to see that she was standing, though she was covered in dust.

"Yes, I'm fine," Mom said. "Luckily there aren't many rocks here."

"What happened?" I asked.

"Goober bucked. I think something scared him. He was behaving so well that it totally took me by surprise. It wasn't even a bad buck. I think he kicked me while running away. My butt is sore, and not from landing on it."

Over the next few days, a horseshoe-shaped bruise emerged on my mom's rear end. This was evidence that she was, indeed, training a young horse.

To make for a softer landing, the next couple of times Goober had a rider on, we took him into the lake. With the resistance of the water, Goober couldn't run as fast, and with the water coming up almost to his withers, it was a very soft landing in case there were any unplanned dismounts.

At first he would just accompany Barrak and I, along with Midnite and Boogsy. Goober loved to swim, and he would follow right behind our two horses. We didn't even have him on a lead. We had given him the nickname "Moosey," because when Goober was swimming, he looked like a moose following behind our two horses.

Once we had waded into a deeper section of the lake, my dad hopped on Goober bareback. Just like all the other times we'd taken Goober swimming, he seemed perfectly content to follow Boogsy and Midnite, even with someone on his back. We had fun, cooling off and feeling the water between our bare toes. However, as my dad's toes appeared, poking up out of the water, Goober spooked and took off bucking. My dad slid off of his wet back and landed gently in the water.

We only had one more incident with Goober, when Midnite's droppings floated to the top of the lake and spooked him. Before long, though, my dad was riding him again, and felt very comfortable on the young horse. The water helped reduce the impact that riding on hard ground would have had on his joints.

A couple of years after we got Goober, when I was 12, I finally competed in the Tevis Cup. It had felt like an eternity to finally be old enough. Barrak had already ridden it twice, and Tevis was one of the only things my family talked about as the race drew nearer.

There is something magical about the Tevis. It is unlike any other race in the world. There is a 24-hour time limit for the race over the Sierras—the maximum time it would have taken the miners to complete the 100-mile trek. It starts at 5:15 AM in Truckee, California. The trail traverses a series of narrow, winding trails along dramatic drop-offs, steep climbs, and deep canyons, making its way to the Gold Country Fairgrounds in Auburn, California, also known as the endurance capital of the world.

Starting in the dark and ending in the dark, the race is always run on a full moon between July and August. The hottest time of the year only adds to the challenge of the race. It can't be held any earlier because of the amount of snow in the high country, and any later in the year would limit the daylight.

It is crucial to choose a well-trained and experienced steed. The excitement and anxiety of Tevis often gets to many horses, causing health issues. Many horses are pulled out of competition at the first two vet checks due to metabolic problems. Weeding out a lot of novice horses before the race helps reduce some drama. The horses need to meet race qualifications and be at least six years old. Riders under the age of 18 have to be accompanied by an adult over the age of 21 for the entirety of the race.

The Tevis trail is tough. It has 17,040 feet of elevation gain and 21,790 feet of descent. As if climbing to the peak of the Watson Monument—past the Olympic ski area and under ski lifts—wasn't enough, traversing three rugged canyons and wading through the American River provides additional challenges. Even though there is more elevation loss than gain, that doesn't mean it is easier; going up requires more cardiovascular exertion, but the downhills are more demanding on the joints, tendons, and different muscles in the horses' bodies. "Easy" is the last word anyone would use to describe this race. The difficulty and prestige often made it a "bucket list" ride, and one that I was excited to attempt myself.

It was my first 100-mile race. I don't think anything could have prepared me for that race except jumping in feet first. I wanted to ride Midnite but, even though she did great at local races, we were worried she wouldn't handle the California heat too well. My dad let me ride his horse, Taii Myr, a safe but fiery animal that loved to go.

My first Tevis matured me more than all the years of getting up early to milk goats, doing farm chores, and riding horses ever could. I was elated to be able to experience it with my whole family.

Barrak was riding Emmers, and despite our two horses being hot and wanting to go faster, we entertained each other for the first 25 miles. Us two youngsters were just happy to be able to ride alongside our parents in the most historic endurance race in the world. Barrak and I were joking about going faster and winning someday and weren't too concerned about the narrow trails. We were enjoying the scenery and the power of our horses.

However, the wind was sucked out of our sails as we prepared to climb Cougar Rock. I was so excited to have my very
own picture of me and Taii Myr climbing the symbol of the Tevis
Cup. Cougar Rock is an icon of the ride, and I remembered the
awe I felt seeing Dolly's photos of her and her stallion on Cougar
Rock. I wanted to have my own photo just like hers. I felt that if
you didn't cross Cougar Rock, you had cheated Tevis.

The horse in front of us had just reached the summit and
dipped out of sight. Barrak gave Emmers the signal to begin
his ascent. Just as they were getting ready to start climbing, the
horse in front of us balked and backed into view again. The rider
had dismounted and before I even knew what was happening,
the horse backed right off the top of Cougar Rock.

As if in slow motion, it took the horse a few seconds, flipping
in the air, to fall the 30 feet to the bypass trail below. Landing
on its back and neck, the horse continued to flip and roll farther down the steep hillside. It was obvious that it wouldn't sur-
vive. Thankfully, the rider had dismounted as soon as the horse
balked and was physically unharmed. However, the emotional
damage would remain with everyone who had been at the scene.

All four of us dismounted and offered to help, but there was
nothing we could do. With riders coming up behind us, a traffic
jam would only cause more chaos and potential accidents. So we
led our horses around Cougar Rock, on the bypass trail.

My family didn't have much to say about the incident. Even
though we later learned that the horse had a neurological condition and the fall wasn't related to the Tevis trail, the accident set
a somber mood for the next several miles.

As we rode deeper into the Sierras, I struggled with the
heat and humidity. Taii Myr was in amazing shape, and since
I weighed basically nothing, I didn't have to worry about him
once. We went slowly, since we wanted to finish as a family.

That Tevis was my first experience riding over 55 miles. The first few miles in the dark dragged on and on, seeming endless. I had no idea where the trail was going. At one point the trail narrowed, revealing the American River almost directly below us. The full moon illuminated the path and hillside into a perfect grayscale scene. My legs were exhausted, and my mom's horse was beginning to get tired.

The horse Mom was riding was young and, like Goober, could sometimes be clumsy. I was worried that he would step off the trail. I had never noticed steep trails before, or distrusted a horse to misplace their foot, but after watching the horse back off of Cougar Rock, I now feared the narrow trails with steep drop-offs.

I asked my parents if we could walk on foot for a while. They agreed, and we slowly made our way down the nerve-wracking section of trail. I would have been content to walk the next 20 miles to the finish line on foot, but then we would have never made the cut-off times.

Barrak and I tried to distract ourselves from the darkness, humming songs and making up a few stories. The magic of Tevis sucked me deeper into its spell; the full moon and the unity with Taii Myr were enthralling. As the night grew longer and the saddle rubs bigger, we finally rounded a bend to see the spotlight illuminating the 85-mile vet check: Francisco's.

The only thing worse than watching a horse die in front of my eyes at 12 years old was finding out that I wouldn't be finishing my first Tevis alongside my brother and best friend. Emmers had a sore foot, and the vets pulled him. As much as it pained us to leave Barrak behind, we were worried about the cut-off times, and my parents and I continued down the trail. It felt like we were on the wagon train bound for Oregon, and we had to go on without Barrak.

Coming across the America River for the first time was a

memory I will never forget. The volunteers, partying and cheering us on as they asked for our rider numbers, gave us a second wind. It also grounded us that we weren't alone in the world after riding in the still darkness, with only the faint rush of the river and the soft hoofbeats on the dusty trail.

The aisle where the horses were meant to cross was marked with green glow sticks. They were spaced out and illuminated a clear path across the river. Taii Myr didn't hesitate, marching straight into the cool water and taking a long drink. As we began to ford the river, the water rushed into my running shoes, relieving my hot, aching feet. The moon illuminated the valley, and the smell of willows and night permeated the air.

As we made our way across the river towards the single-lane dirt road, I felt ready to get my Tevis buckle. The dirt road was a refreshing break from the narrow trails we had been riding on. I just kept posting, expecting to see the final vet check around every corner.

With six miles to go, we entered the final stop. The once-hot California air had chilled me, my wet, soggy feet dropping my core temperature. I placed a fleece blanket on Taii Myr to keep his muscles warm. The volunteers kept us moving along as we stressed about the cut-off time. We would have plenty of time if we kept moving at the pace we were going, but we couldn't go any slower or spend any extra time at the vet stop. My mom's horse was also getting tired, so we couldn't go much faster, either.

Leaving Lower Quarry with my parents, Taii Myr felt as strong as ever, and led the way to Auburn. Crossing No Hands Bridge, I could hardly hold in my excitement about actually riding Tevis. I wanted to canter across the bridge with my arms stretched out to my sides. Instead, we slowly trotted across it, the horses' hooves clopping against the cement as the shadow of the historic bridge reflected against the American River way below.

My excitement didn't last long, and I tried my best to stay awake. I had never stayed up that late before, and the exhausting day in the saddle brought sleep eagerly knocking at my door. I caught my head nodding a couple of times. I tried talking out loud, telling myself that we only had a few more miles to go.

The last four miles felt about as long as the first 25, but a little after 3:00 AM, we rounded the final bend of the Tevis trail. The incline leading to the finish line seemed so short as Taii Myr plowed his way up the hill and under the banner. Crossing the stadium banner with my parents by my side, hand in hand, was one of the best moments of my life.

I had never been so sore. My shoulders and arms felt like I had been run over by a car from holding Taii Myr back for the first half of the race. My legs and calves were so sore and chafed that I could barely get into the backseat of the pick-up. I couldn't use my arms to pull myself up, and my legs had no suspension left in them. Before long, my cheeks hurt, too, because I couldn't stop smiling. I was elated. It was all too much for my 12-year-old brain to process, and sleep came within seconds of me inviting it in.

The exhaustion of being on the trail for 22 hours straight toughened me right up. I learned to kick sleep away and push on, only occasionally giving in and dozing off while riding my horse at three o'clock in the morning. Even with the horrible accident on the trail that day and my own hesitations, we still finished in 42nd place. After that, I proudly wore the belt buckle I had won with every pair of jeans, every day. It read: "Western States Trail Ride – 100 miles – One Day."

I was happy, but still aching for something more. I had my heart set on racing in the front, not in the middle of the pack.

CHAPTER 4

Goober's First Race

Over the next few years, Goober hovered between the cute baby stage and being a grown horse. He was growing physically, but he was still a big goofball and immature as ever.

In the summers, we turned Goober loose on nearby pastures. While he ran around and grew stronger, Midnite and I raced across the West Coast. We weren't content with just finishing, though; we wanted to go fast and win, even competing against adults and more seasoned riders we were able to accomplish that.

During the winters, while our racehorses enjoyed a break from training, we spent time working with the youngsters and began the early training stages of Goober's endurance career. We conditioned the herd by running them around the border of their oval pen for an hour a couple of times a week. The horses ran between the outside fence and a makeshift rail we hung up using baling twine tied to trees. Our horses' unique personalities came out during this process (called penning). The competitive ones galloped and raced for the front, and the lazy ones hid behind trees and hoped you wouldn't notice them. Goober enjoyed exercising and wanted to be towards the pack's head, but the veteran racehorses made him stay in the back, so he would often just duck under the string and cut corners.

Goober's life of freedom slowly came to an end during his fourth year. It was now time to prepare him for his future as an endurance racehorse. It takes a long time to bring a horse up. Many horses come into the sport strong, race for a few years, and end up lame and have to retire early because of too much pressure too soon. Having a good horse is not enough; you have to have patience and bring them up correctly.

Standing just under 16 hands (or about 64 inches from the ground to the top of his withers), Goober was showing a lot of potential. The first few months of riding him were mainly refreshers and saddle training. Once Goober got the hang of riding and didn't buck, we began to condition him. For him, training rides were a walk in the park. He had a lot of natural talent, and the winter penning helped give him a solid base.

Goober was easygoing on the trail, preferring to follow the other horses. When he was in the front of the pack, he was on high alert and would spook at anything that might endanger him and his friends, such as scary tree stumps that could be mistaken for a predator. It got a little frustrating, but we understood that he wanted to protect his herd. The horse in the front feels the most responsibility to protect the horses in tow.

During training, Goober showed promise. We started him young and soon had high hopes for him. He had phenomenally low heart rate readings, and his recoveries were outstanding. After a hard training ride, his heart rate would drop back down very quickly. When he was five years old, we began conditioning him for his first race season. He was developing nicely, and by the time the 2014 season opened up in the Northwest region, we had signed up for our first race in April.

I wouldn't be racing Midnite during Goober's first race. Instead, I'd be supervising Goober with a perfect Arabian gelding named Focus Farino. It was also Focus's first race, but he was older than Goober and a lot more trained.

There comes a point when a horse has taught you all they

can, and to improve as a rider, you need to find another mount that will challenge you. I had outgrown Midnite in my ability and was ready for a horse that would test me. Midnite was more of a babysitter, and I wanted a hot, energetic horse full of spice and fire. I was helping my parents train some of their "investment" horses; compared to calm and steady Midnite, they seemed so exciting and challenging. I had an unbreakable bond with Midnite, but I slowly stopped enjoying riding her as much as I did some of the other horses we had, like Focus.

The first ride we attended during the 2014 season was about 30 minutes from our home. Most riders came from quite a ways away and camped out at the start of the ride. We slept better in our own beds, so if the ride was within a reasonable driving distance, we always chose to arrive the morning of the race instead. Endurance rides start as early as possible because it will be such a long day on the trail, and you want to finish before dark. Usually, 50-mile races begin at around 6:00 AM.

Shortly after being awoken at 4:00 by the screeching alarm, the house bustled as we did some last-minute packing and coffee-brewing. We then headed into the dark to load the four horses into the trailer, hitting the empty road and driving the half-hour to the endurance ride camp.

Trailers were scattered through the sagebrush. We recognized some as serious competition from other races, and others belonged to people we hadn't seen in a while. We were looking forward to the opportunity to catch up with them. My dad and Barrak were on Pre and Emmers, two more experienced horses, and would be competing to win. I was signed up to ride Focus and accompany my mom, who would be on Goober. Since it was the first race for the horses Mom and I were riding, we had planned to not get caught up in the competition, but rather simply to try to finish. We wanted to introduce our horses to the commotion of a race and show them what it meant to work in a competition.

This race was called the Grizzly Mountain Ride, beginning at the base of Grizzly Butte. It has a couple of nice inclines but is a pretty flat ride overall. Because of the terrain, we could usually put down some pretty good times with seasoned horses. The first race of the season is always a little more nerve-racking than the rest. However, it is a good indicator of how well the training progressed over the winter and where your horse stands.

We unloaded our four horses. Excited whinnies filled the cold morning air. The sun had yet to rise and bring its light and warmth to the endurance camp, but the whole settlement was awake. People were rushing back and forth, getting their horses' electrolytes, feeding them their morning grain, and making breakfast for themselves.

Mom went to the registration desk, filled out the papers, and brought us our vet cards, which we had to give to the vet to fill out during our mandatory holds and vet checks. We untied the horses we would be riding from the trailer and made our way to where the vet was still waking up. Following the pre-race vet examination, we tacked up our horses with minimal race gear, trying to keep it as light as possible.

"Do you guys all have an Easyboot?" Pa asked before every ride. Easyboots are like spare tires. If your horse loses a shoe on rocky ground, you are basically out of the race, so we always carried an Easyboot—a rubber boot that fits over the horse's hoof and has a couple wires to secure it. It is better to have it and not need it than not have it when you do need it.

The pre-race commotion intensified as we rushed around,

putting leg-protection boots on our horses, tightening girths, getting some last-minute drinks of water, and shoving energy bars into our pockets. The horses sensed the excitement and, despite being tied to the trailer, pranced in place.

Soon after my mom mounted Goober, he lost it. All the excitement and commotion and screaming horses had worked him up, but it was the noise of a big Canadian flag whipping in the wind that got to him, resulting in a colossal meltdown. Goober didn't want to calm down, and my mom and dad quickly switched saddles. That was the last time he was considered Mom's horse.

Goober still had some fits while we were warming up, but six and a half hours later and 50 miles down the road, he wasn't even thinking about misbehaving. He had good vet scores and his recoveries were impressive, but his lack of motivation after he finally settled down made us wonder if he would have enough drive to be a champion.

The first race of the season was a success for my family. Goober impressed us with his fast recoveries and raw talent, and Focus stole my heart and quickly became my favorite horse. Barrak won the race, with mom right behind in 2nd, proving that their horses were ready to take on the Tevis Cup four months later.

The Tevis Cup is to endurance racing what the Kentucky Derby is to track racing. We used the local races as training for Tevis, which is like the Tour de France of endurance. It is the most challenging equestrian endurance race in North America, and arguably in the world.

After Emmers' impressive performance at the Grizzly Mountain ride, we were optimistic for his run at Tevis. When Emmers was having a good day, nothing could stand in his way. He was the kind of horse that would either win or get eliminated. He and Barrak had raced Tevis twice before.

A good friend of ours, Pat Richardson, had given Emmers to us a few years earlier, when she got out of horses; she knew we would try to bring out the best in him. He had enormous feet that were somewhat sensitive and often had abscesses or bruises. He was 16.3 hands tall and probably close to 1,200 pounds, which is quite large for a purebred Arabian. He didn't show much promise for longer distances and had a lot of pulls on his race record. Several people discouraged us by saying he would never make a 100-mile race without going lame. After his two Tevis pulls, we were beginning to wonder if they were right.

The first time Emmers and Barrak attempted Tevis, when I was 11 years old, I was sure they were going to finish in the top 10. I refreshed the webcast every few minutes, anticipating their arrival in Auburn.

I couldn't hear who was on the other end of the line, but I knew that the caller didn't have good news from the way my mom's face fell. My parents got the heartbreaking call that Barrak and Emmers had been pulled at Lower Quarry, six miles from the finish. They had been running in the top 10 all day and were so close to finishing. After my dad had been pulled earlier in the race, Garrett and Lisa Ford had graciously sponsored Barrak for the majority of the race.

The next year, Barrak and I rode Tevis for the first time together. I was overjoyed to be riding alongside my parents and Barrak for the first 85 miles. At Francisco's, Emmers had problems with his feet again and was pulled. Although I had the thrill of finishing side by side with my parents, I missed having my brother and Emmers in my first Tevis finish photo.

In 2014, I took a break from racing Tevis because of the

traumatic mishap that had happened at Cougar Rock. Although some freak accidents do occasionally occur at Tevis, no riders have ever died during the race, and it is extremely seldom for a horse to be fatally injured. However, despite the slim chances of a horse dying on the trail, this particular incident had happened right in front of me. For a while I denied that it had affected me, but it certainly had. I have a horrific fear of drop-offs and riding on narrow trails; I can picture the horse I'm riding falling down the hillside the way that horse did at Tevis, getting tangled in the vegetation only to free itself and then roll farther down the hillside.

Whenever possible, I always choose to avoid steep trails. Even on reliable horses, I get nervous and sometimes walk them by hand along the steep sections of trail. As often as I tell myself that my horse will do everything in its power to stay alive and keep all four hooves on the trail, I still have this phobia.

So, as much as I wanted to race competitively at Tevis, I needed to regain my confidence on narrow trails. Even though I wasn't riding in the competition myself, it was just as exciting to be part of the support crew for my parents and Barrak. Waiting at the 68-mile vet stop at Forest Hill, I played cards in the baking California sun with the other crew members. Every few minutes I would refresh the live standing following my family member's progress. Between card games, I would double-check to make sure we had everything lined and ready for when our riders arrived.

I'll never forget the thrill of my brother and mom entering the 68-mile vet stop, within striking distance of the top 10 horses. As they left the vet stop, riding into the setting sun with another 36 miles to go, I refreshed the feed more frequently, the suspense rising. They slowly moved up positions, and I didn't need to ride with them to feel the pride of having my family finish in the top

10 in the Tevis Cup.

Barrak proved everyone wrong who had doubted his horse Emmers, finishing not just any 100-mile race, but the most challenging one in 7th place on their third attempt. As exciting as it had been to watch the Haggin Cup judging the first time around, it couldn't compare to the pride of watching a family member present their horse.

The suspense of knowing that Barrak had a chance of winning—but also trying not to get our hopes up—was killing me as the winner was about to be announced. I didn't realize that I was holding my breath as the head veterinarian announced, "The winner of the 2014 James Ben Ali Haggin Cup is . . . MCM Last Dance, ridden by Barrak Blakeley."

I never could have imagined that, seven years after witnessing my first Haggin Cup judging the morning after my parents' first Tevis, someone in my family would win the very prestigious Best Condition award at Tevis! It was the first time a winner had finished in the top 10 with a horse that was older than the rider. At the time, Barrak was 15 years old, and Emmers was 17. Everybody loved that, and Barrak quickly became well known for being the youngest rider with the oldest horse to win the Haggin Cup.

Witnessing Barrak's achievement, I caught the bug to try riding Tevis again. It made my goal of placing in the top 10 seem achievable.

CHAPTER 5

My Heart Horse

Over the years, we have trained and raced a lot of different horses. Over 50 of them have come and gone through our stables.

Each horse brings something unique and leaves with a piece of you. Saying goodbye is never easy, but it is part of the business. We are constantly sifting through horses, trying to bring out the best in each one.

Into our evolving herd came a gelding that changed my life and carried a large piece of my heart. His name was Focus Farino. I'm not sure why Focus left a more profound impression than so many others, but he did. He was beautiful, personable, and a joy to be around. Letting go of Midnite was the hardest thing I had done up until then, and Focus was the only thing that made it easier. The night before Midnite was to be picked up, I snuck out of the house in the dark and buried my face in her mane. She didn't know why I was so upset as I cradled her neck around my sobbing body. Her big bug eyes, which held so much love, looked worried; she didn't know how to comfort me. I felt like I had let her down.

Midnite was the first horse I ever cried over, and the first horse that carried a large piece of my heart with her to her new home in California, where she would steal another kid's heart.

We bought Focus because he was a good Craigslist buy. At first, we viewed him as an investment. Factors such as age, height, bloodlines, race record, and a few other things determine a horse's value; a good horse can sell for a better price if they are between six and ten years old, are taller than 15.1 hands (5 foot, 1 inch), and have done a few races.

Focus was seven years old, a prime age, and at 15.3 hands, he was the ideal height for an endurance horse. And he was absolutely beautiful. He was a leggy chestnut gelding with lots of chrome—distinctive white markings that set him apart. He had three tall stockings on his legs and a perfect blaze on his forehead. His blaze started out round and tapered down to his muzzle, like a teardrop dripping down his face in perfect symmetry. I had a browband on my bridle that was silver-plated, with a "V" right in the center. The V covered the top of his blaze, forming a perfect heart shape.

Focus was the kind of horse that could cheer me up after a tough day at school. He always looked like he was smiling and happy to see me. He would nuzzle my pockets for treats and wrap his neck around me, giving me horse hugs. Despite Focus being forward and hot, I was never scared of him running away with me, even if my arms throbbed from keeping him under control.

During the race season, training can become routine and exhausting. To keep ourselves engaged and focused on the fun part of having horses, my family and I would occasionally go horse camping. Camping out for the weekend at Henderson Flats, we spent the majority of the day in the hills, where we often trained the horses but enjoyed the slower pace of exploring ravines and valleys.

Barrak and I galloped our horses through the hills with no saddle, just a halter and reins. I was riding my Focus, and Barrak was on Pre, one of our other horses. What Focus was to Midnite, Pre was to Boogsy. The pair tested our abilities and helped us grow as riders.

We weaved through the familiar hollows on Focus and Pre, hiding clues for my parents to find in our traditional family treasure hunt. We hid clues all over the hills—in an old rotten tree, under huge rocks—with vague hints that would lead my parents to one of the springs trickling down a ravine, which you could only discover by a cow trail. After riding all day and following clues, the hunt led my parents back to our camp to find the treasure of chocolate coins hidden in the horse trailer. Our treasure hunt bonded us.

Focus loved me, too. He was naturally a more nervous horse, but my fearlessness and confidence pushed him through anything. He was my Hidalgo. He had the sweetest personality and always wanted to please me. His previous owner had taught him to lie down, so I often asked him to do so and then climbed up on his back. Focus had no flaws, but then again, I am biased.

At one point, we tried our hand at jumping. Barrak and I made a couple of jumps with old lumber we found lying around the property. We cut a small sheet of plywood into the stand and used two-by-six planks for the base. We bent 16 penny nails driven into the plywood as our hangers, measured out every 6 inches. Barrak painted the jump blue with red stripes. He was always an artist. I painted the PVC pipe red, since there weren't too many ways I could ruin the design.

We set up our homemade jump in the pasture and, without a saddle or bridle, we hopped on Focus and Pre to warm them up. We cantered them around the pasture a few times. Once we felt comfortable with our horses, I watched Barrak go first with Pre to test our jump. We started jumping at six inches, and Pre easily cleared it. I cantered Focus over, and he was enthusiastic and coordinated. After making sure the horses were comfortable at 6 inches, we moved it up to a foot.

The first jump at a foot was a little more strenuous without a saddle. Focus was getting really into jumping and clearing it with plenty of room. We kept moving the PVC pipe up on our bent nails, six inches at a time, until we made it to three feet.

Three feet was about as high as our jump would go, since the plywood wasn't much taller and the weight of the PVC pipe would have pulled the light jump right over. I am sure Focus and Pre could have jumped higher, had we given them the opportunity.

The longer and more often I jumped Focus, the more I had to hold on with my knees and concentrate on balancing. Focus enjoyed himself so much that he gave little consideration to the rope halter I was riding him in. Though it was meant to slow him down, he only got faster and faster. After every jump, it took longer to get him back into a trot to ride back to the other side of the jump. On our last jump, I seriously reconsidered my lack of brakes; Focus didn't slow down after we cleared the jump, and kept running full speed towards the pasture fence. Worried that he would try jumping the pasture fence, too, I put all my lightweight into one rein to pull him into a single-rein stop. I finally slowed him down before he launched us over the corral fence.

I hopped off my hot, beautiful horse and ran to the trailer to get a bridle. As I was grabbing one, my mom called us for lunch. We put the horses back and set our cheesy jump aside, planning to come back to it soon. But that was the last time I jumped Focus bareback.

Since my family isn't wealthy and horses are expensive, we always had to sell a couple of horses each year to afford the upkeep of the others. Two things about being in the horse business: 1) Everybody knows your best horses, and 2) You have to sell them to pay for the others.

In 2014, our only two horses that were worth enough to cover the year's expenses were Goober and Focus. We advertised

Goober for sale and had a lot of interest in him from all over the country and even from international buyers. Potential buyers from Texas, Southern California, Arizona, and overseas were interested in the flashy, dark bay up-and-comer that had completed a couple of races and even won a "Best Condition" award in his first year of racing.

We wrote paragraph after paragraph in long emails, answering questions, describing our horses, and responding to endless requests for videos. People constantly requested videos and photos of a horse doing this and that. There were a lot of tire kickers who never responded, after we put so much effort into communicating with them.

By the time we were done dealing with people picking our dear horses apart, we almost wanted to pay somebody to take them off our hands, even though they were still top-quality horses. We had several serious inquiries about Goober, but after we sent many videos to multiple interested parties, they all criticized him for one reason or another.

"He is lame on his left front leg."

"He's lame on his right front."

"He ropewalks."

"I don't want to buy him; he looks like he paddles."

Goober was most certainly *not* lame on either side, and he did not ropewalk or paddle (both of which are irregular strides). The more time we spent with Goober, taking videos and pictures, and the less people wanted him, the more we appreciated him and realized what a talented horse he was.

We had several positive potential buyers as well. One woman liked everything about Goober and offered a competitive home that would help promote him to the top. After corresponding back and forth, she scheduled an appointment for a pre-purchase examination with the Bend Equine Veterinary Clinic.

Several days before the exam, Goober was getting new shoes and was trimmed too short. He came up lame, so we ended up canceling his appointment. He was fine a few days later; he just wasn't ready to leave yet.

Nobody could find anything wrong with Focus, and he sold for a nice price to the first person who expressed interest. Even though he wasn't part of the herd for very long, I loved Focus. There have been only four horses I've cried over when we had to let them go, and he was one of them. After Midnite, Focus was the second.

In a perfect world, I would still have Focus. But the world isn't perfect, and I had to let him go. Through the sale of my handsome boy, we were able to afford to fill the barn with hay and cover our expenses for the year. The only thing that brought me comfort was that at least we were able to keep Goober.

I said goodbye to Focus through a haze of tears as he headed to Texas, where he would be quarantined in an isolated stall for a couple of weeks to ensure that he wouldn't take any diseases or sicknesses with him overseas. Once his time in quarantine was up, he boarded a plane bound for his new family in Abu Dhabi.

Focus's new owner, Veronica, a veterinarian from Spain, kept us updated on how he was doing. She sent pictures of his stall, which had air conditioning and other amenities that some humans didn't even get to enjoy. He was signed up for his first 80-kilometer (50-mile) qualifier race in Abu Dhabi about six months after arriving there. We received the email announcement of his upcoming race while we were visiting family in Germany.

"How often are you only a $250 flight away from Dubai?" Pa said. "Maybe we can swing it."

My parents looked closely at the budget for the next couple of months and decided what we could live without in order to make a quick trip to the Middle East. At the time, we didn't have the money for trips like that. We couldn't even afford to buy the flights to Germany, but my parents had accumulated air miles from their credit cards to help swing the visit. Spending time with my mom's side of the family and getting to know Germany was very important to my parents in educating my brother and I. They felt that traveling, keeping up with our second language, and being immersed in a different culture was more important than a textbook education. They also believed that memories were more valuable than having a nice car or name-brand clothes.

We agreed that this was a once-in-a-lifetime opportunity, so we bought the tickets and hoped we wouldn't have many expenses. My parents had maxed out their credit cards.

The day before our flight to Dubai, my 88-year-old German grandma slipped trying to catch the bus and broke her femur. She needed surgery and was confined to a hospital bed, so of course I felt we would need to stay with her and miss out on the opportunity to see Focus.

"Just go," Grandma told us, "and promise you'll bring me back an Arab scarf. *Geh mit Gott, aber geh.*" She said she would feel horrible having us stay behind for her, especially since there wasn't anything we could do for her in the hospital.

We planned to go for only four days. The next morning, we were on a flight from Germany bound for the Middle East. Based on our research on the internet, we were prepared to land in a strict Muslim country. I packed very modest clothes: oversized jeans and long-sleeved T-shirts.

We had to change planes in Moscow and arrived in Dubai on the day of Focus's race. The lines in customs were atrociously long, despite it being two hours after midnight. The crowds included lots of people coming from less affluent Asian countries to work in the wealthy United Arab Emirates.

English was not Veronica's first language, and that caused a bit of confusion for us, as her emails were always a little vague. In fact, we had believed Focus was going to live in Spain, Veronica's home country, when we sold him to her.

When we arrived in Dubai, there was a message from Veronica that said simply: "Khamis, my fiancé's brother, will pick you up at the airport at around 5:00 AM at Costa Coffee."

After over three hours in customs, we waited at Costa Coffee for a guy named Khamis. Unfortunately, we had no description to go by, only a name, so we bought coffee and waited. I scoffed at a sign covering part of the airport that was under renovation: "Sorry for the inconvenience. We are working on creating the best airport in the world."

"Is everything bigger in the UAE?" I joked.

"Yep," Barrak said. "Biggest building, biggest airplane, and even the biggest indoor aquarium. So yeah, just about everything is bigger in Dubai."

The wall clock read 6:00.

"Can you call Veronica and see if Khamis is still coming?" Pa asked my mom.

Mom looked at her phone. "I don't have any cell service. And the airport Wi-Fi is overloaded."

At a quarter to seven and still no Khamis, we ordered a second coffee.

"What if he doesn't show up?" I asked.

"Well, I guess we can always find a hotel and maybe contact them from there," my dad said.

"Worse comes to worst, we can have a lovely vacation in Dubai without seeing any horses." My mom liked to bring up the positive in any situation. We looked and felt out of place, the four of us wearing our matching "Blakeley Stables" T-shirts, waiting in a coffee shop for someone we didn't know.

At around 7:00 AM, a young man with a well-trimmed beard came up to our table.

"Hi, I'm Khamis," he said. "You must be Focus' family."

"Yes, thank you for picking us up and letting us come visit," Pa said, shaking his hand.

After introductions, Khamis brought us back to reality. "We have to get going. The race will start soon, and it is a couple of hours from here."

It didn't take long to befriend Khamis as we rode in his Toyota SUV, destined for the endurance village. He was easy to talk to and went out of his way for guests, explaining the sights along the way. Leaving the city and driving through the desert made us feel as though we were on Mars. There were no trees or vegetation. Instead, there were gigantic rusty dunes and alien-looking camels wandering the roads.

"This is Focus's family from America," Veronica said as she introduced us to fellow endurance racers around the village. Veronica's fiancé, Rashid, was riding Focus on his first race. They had nicknamed him "Crazy Horse" because he loved to go fast and perhaps lacked a little brake fluid.

UAE racing seemed like more of an art than what we did at home. The horses imported to the UAE were putting down some crazy fast times. The Middle East is always the top contender at the World Equestrian Games. That part of the world is consistently setting new speed records. The United Arab Emirates holds the world record for completing 100 miles in 5 hours and 45 minutes. That is maintaining an 18-miles-an-hour gallop for 100 miles.

Focus made us proud. I was so happy to see him again, and

he seemed happy to see me too. Unlike the trails in the United States, the race course in Abu Dhabi is carved into the sand. With twin lanes running parallel to the horses, the crew follows along in two vehicles. They carry water bottles and, regularly, the team (mainly Indian and Pakistani stable hands) hands the riders the bottles, which they empty on the horses as they continue galloping along.

After the race, Focus's legs were iced, and his back poulticed and massaged. Al Raad Stable treated its horses like kings. There was no care lacking. Rashid and Veronica showed us around the stable and introduced us to their herd. Each stall contained a horse from a different part of the world—Focus from the U.S., Ameer from Spain, and others from France, Uruguay, and Australia.

Many of the world's best horses end up in the UAE. Because there aren't any pastures in that environment, the UAE doesn't breed endurance horses. Instead, stables import their horses and their food. Importing everything drives up the cost of feeding and housing a horse. So, not just any horse goes there; mainly those worth the investment, with the potential to be a champion.

We ended our day with a gorgeous boat ride up one of the city canals, the warm yellow city lights reflecting off the black water. The scent of dates and palm trees permeated the air. Street performers walked the banks of the canals, and the smell of freshly cooked bread and curries wafted around us. Meandering through the beautiful city, we felt out of place in our modest clothes. Women wearing short-shorts and tight jeans reflected the strong Western influence in Dubai.

Our new friends didn't withhold any hospitality at dinner. We enjoyed a multi-course meal of outstanding Middle Eastern dishes, and then we were transported back to our comfortable hotel.

The next morning, Khamis picked us up again for a day of racing. Unlike the day before, Al Raad's endurance team tried to place better with Vesuvio, their more seasoned horse, so we were watching horses we didn't really know.

Endurance racing can be boring for spectators, but watching horses at these much faster speeds made it more interesting. During the holds, we shared a camel milk tea drink, sitting on Persian rugs with pillows to lean on, and waited for the horses to finish each loop.

During the break, Veronica took us to meet some camels.

"Can we ride them?" my dad asked the herder.

"No, no," the man replied, shaking his head vigorously.

"Please, can we ride your camels?" Pa asked again.

"No, no, no," the man said again. "You no ride camels."

"Are you sure? We can pay you to ride the camels. You don't come to a country with camels everywhere and not ride one."

"No, you pet camels, but no ride," the man repeated.

It was clear that we would have had a better chance of riding a camel back home at the local fair. We settled for just a picture instead, then got back into Veronica's car to follow Vesuvio for his final loop.

"Do you know why they wouldn't let us ride the camels?" my dad asked Veronica.

"I think some of the camels carry diseases," was the best she could come up with.

All at once, the jet lag finally caught up to me. I gave in to sleep in the back seat of Veronica's car, enjoying the air conditioning and waking up just in time to see the finish.

That evening, back at the stables, Veronica and Rashid let me and Barrak ride two of their best horses. I got to ride Faramia, their most valuable horse. Riding her was 100 times better than riding a camel. As the gray mare carried me through the sea of sand, Rashid drove his SUV alongside the riders, instructing us how exactly to condition the horses. He told us when to switch gaits and leads.

"Now gallop on the left lead," he told us after we had trotted a bit. About a mile later, he instructed everybody to switch to the horse's right lead. The coordination and methods of training put these horses on a more competitive and professional level of racing.

Coming back from our ride, the grooms took care of our horses, and Veronica drew the horses' blood. Unfortunately, the results showed that one of the horses was missing some crucial minerals. Within minutes, Veronica had adjusted his training plan and administered the needed minerals through an IV. Medication and various nutrients filled the stable's refrigerated feed room. There were supplements we had never heard of before, as well as high-tech laboratory machines, all in the same room as the hay imported from Texas.

After an evening of chatting with our fellow horse enthusiasts, Barrak and I headed to the rooftop of our hotel for a midnight swim in the saltwater pool under a star-filled sky, with Dubai's city lights in the distance.

On our way to the airport the next day, we took some time to visit a few more highlights of Dubai. The Burj Khalifa, the world's tallest building, was just as impressive in daylight as it was lit up at night. Our last stop before the airport was the Dubai mall. We bought a silk scarf for my grandma and smelled a lot of different Arabic perfumes worth thousands of dollars.

Overall, it was a fantastic trip. The culture we explored was fascinating, and our new friends inspired us in our resolve to challenge our horses to new limits and dive deeper into the world of competitive endurance racing. Even though it was hard to see Focus in anybody's barn but ours, I didn't think he could have a much better home. In the care of Veronica and Rashid, his potential as a world-class athlete would be reached.

CHAPTER 6

Goober's First 100-Mile Race

After we sold Focus, my parents let me ride Goober. He helped mend the hole in my heart that Focus had left, and I enjoyed riding him. In 2015, his second season, he won a race and placed in the top 10 in his next three 50-mile races with my dad.

Since I was only 14 at the time and weighed significantly less than Pa, it seemed like a reasonable choice that I would pilot Goober through his first 100-mile ride. The less weight a horse is carrying, the easier it is for them, especially if they have been used to training with more weight. At races we always tried to keep our tack and load as light as possible, only carrying what was absolutely necessary. A lot of competitive riders used saddles made out of carbon fiber that weigh next to nothing. We couldn't afford these saddles (which were more expensive than most of our horses!) and instead race with lightweight synthetic saddles that we found at yard sales.

After my disastrous attempt at Tevis earlier that year, I looked forward to a second chance at finishing a 100-mile race. Barrak had let me ride Pre at Tevis, and I was excited to have finally found the courage to try again after my traumatic experience at my first Tevis. Since Barrak had won the Haggin Cup the year before, I was ready to chase my dream of getting in the top 10 at Tevis, and I felt confident with Pre.

Unfortunately, our race was cut short at 55 miles. Pre wasn't drinking as well as he should have been and got a little dehydrated. Pre and I went from being ready to take on the world to standing utterly defeated in the old ghost town of Deadwood.

I wanted to be sure to be as prepared as possible for my next 100-mile attempt with Goober. My family and I went running quite a bit to keep in good shape for races, and also to keep an eye on our weight to lighten the burden on our horses. There is a common misconception that horseback riders just sit there and let the horse do all the work. That is definitely not true; keeping several endurance horses in top shape kept me in top shape as well.

I had only ridden Goober a handful of times, and I wanted to bond with him before the Oregon 100 race. I took him out to Smith Rocks, a local state park with stunning views and great trails. The Crooked River divides the rock faces that are freckled with rock climbers. I rode Goober by himself to get a good feel for how he was without his friends around and connect with him one-on-one.

After crossing the Crooked River and winding through narrow trails over roots and boulders, Goober and I arrived at the base of a hill called Burma Road. The three switchbacks led us along the rocky road, which climbed about 1,000 feet. Goober, having double the number of legs as the runners, did double the number of hill repeats. So, we went twice up the front side and twice up the back side. I played some jams from my phone as Goober galloped up the gradual inclines, enjoying the kind of music a 14-year-old girl liked in 2015 (probably some Katy Perry, Justin Timberlake, and Adele in the mix).

My first race with Goober would be almost the exact opposite of Tevis. Unlike Tevis, there was practically no elevation change over the whole 100-mile course. It was held just outside a small town called Brothers. If you blinked while driving through, you would miss it. It seemed like there was maybe one tree in about a 25-mile radius, and the smell of sagebrush and dust was the only other thing you noticed. The racecourse is flat and sandy, and it is easy to underestimate the challenge of this course.

After much prepping and anxiety, race day rolled around. We spent the night in the vast desert to be ready before sunrise. The Oregon 100 is one of my all-time favorite rides. Although it is not as scenic as some other rides, I love the desert—the wide open spaces, clear skies, and, at night, penetrating cold. The stars seem closer and shine like billions of diamonds in the sky.

When we camped with the horses, I always set up my foam mattress on the back of our flatbed truck and snuggled into my sleeping bag. I fell asleep to the peaceful sounds of horses munching hay in their pens set up next to the trailer. Since my bed was one boundary of their fence, I sometimes hid treats in my sleeping bag and bribed the horses for cuddles. Curious ones came to nuzzle the top of my head, the only thing showing out of layers of sleeping bags. The downfall was they would then bug me for treats for the rest of the night, preventing my much-needed rest.

I was up before the alarm went off at 4:00 AM, and enjoyed the peaceful, quiet desert morning from the cozy warmth of my sleeping bag. Occasionally, I could hear the distant sound of a long-haul truck rolling down the lonely highway several hundred yards away. As the alarm went off in the trailer's bunk and I heard my parents fumble around for the light, I knew I would have a little more time in my sleeping bag before getting up for the long day ahead of me. The butterflies in my stomach were relentless. I had only completed one 100-mile race before, and

Goober was still a pill at the start of races. A million scenarios crossed my mind as I wondered why I had signed up for this. Worst-case scenarios and what-ifs bounced around in my mind.

My parents rolled out of the trailer and started the small propane camp stove on the trailer's fender to boil water for their coffee. It was still pitch-black except for the light of the stars and tiny rays from their weak headlamps. The kettle's shrill whistle soon ended the silence.

I covered my ears with my hands, which were still warm, and began to shiver. Half of it was nerves, the other half the sub-freezing temperatures. I folded my bed together, knowing that a film of dust would cover anything I left out within a few hours. I quickly tied my running shoes, zipped up my half chaps, and stepped into the heated trailer for a few minutes. I knew if I stayed too long, I would have difficulty peeling myself out when I needed to leave. I pulled out my vet card, with the pre-ride column that had been filled out the night before, and we wrote the loop colors and distances on the top. There were seven vet checks in this race; the first loop was 35 miles long with a trot-by vet check-in at the halfway point, out in the boonies.

The horses were getting antsy. They could sense our excitement. I tried to warm the cold metal bit in my hands before offering it to Goober. I then placed the breast collar gingerly over his ears and snapped it in place to keep the saddle from sliding, then walked through the powdery dirt to the trailer's tack area, where I selected a pair of leg boots. Knowing Goober would go through several pairs that day, I wasn't particular about which ones I put on him first.

I led him around a little and cast my light over all the equipment, making sure I hadn't forgotten anything. Then I asked my mom to hold Goober while I mounted. He began throwing his head as a sign to let him go. I nodded to Mom, letting her know

I could handle him. Goober pranced sideways a few steps and let out a few whinnies before I put him into a controlled trot to warm up his muscles and distract him from the excitement.

My dad and I rode side by side and warmed up the horses' muscles in the dark. Horses see well at night, so we didn't use artificial light because it simply impedes their vision. We trusted our horses' senses over our own in this environment. Then it was time to head back to the volunteers who kept track of race timing. They were in charge of recording the time a rider leaves, and how long they are on the course. Everyone is assigned a rider number to simplify timekeeping.

We arrived at the race start a few minutes early and stood around waiting for the timers to take our numbers. Goober began to get excited, prancing off sideways again. I pressed my calf into his side, attempting to get him to stop, but it didn't help. Instead, he started energetically tossing his head up and down. I knew if I kept fighting him, he would get annoyed and might start bucking, so I released all leg pressure and redirected him down the road with my reins.

I met up with my dad just as the timer announced that the course was open. Trotting off down the dark dirt road, Pa and I were side by side, with several competitors ahead. We had the goal of finishing and didn't want to get caught in the competition. We knew it would be smart to start strong, so the horses wouldn't have too much time to express their energy.

After a couple of miles, my arms began to tire a little from holding Goober back. But even with tired muscles, there is no better feeling than having a powerful horse under you. I was the brain that kept him paced to hold out for 100 miles, and he was the muscle that propelled us all day long.

As the day heated up and the remaining miles decreased, we forged ahead, each stride bringing us closer to the 100-mile goal. The one thing this race had in common with Tevis was the heat. While the heat of the Oregon desert doesn't compare to California, it was unusually hot for September, and with no trees to shade us, we were like lizards baking in the sun. I was beginning to feel the effects of the long day. My lips were chapped and my muscles were throbbing. I now had a dark trail-dust mustache, and the sticky electrolytes mixed with molasses that Goober kept spitting back on me dripped from my hands to my elbows.

At around mile 80, with two loops to go, Goober was still feeling great as the evening breeze kicked in and brought along a fresh wind. To my surprise, we were leading the race; some of the riders who were in the lead at first had taken a wrong turn and ended up behind us. But the competition was closing in.

Riding down roads we had been on previously, we got to the water trough we had ridden past back at mile 20. There was some hay, and the horses were hungry for anything they could get their teeth on. After letting the horses drink their fill, my dad and I each grabbed an armful of the hay and continued walking up the road on foot, letting our horses eat from our armload. It was nice to stretch our legs.

A few hundred yards from the water trough, my dad's horse, Sporty, started to choke on some of the feed. Talk about a panic attack. Pa thrust his hand into the horse's mouth and attempted to dislodge the hay. I handed him my water bottle, and he poured that into his horse's mouth. Green slime came out as he continued to hack. Pa and I watched in terror. We were miles from camp, and his horse was choking.

Sporty is going to die out here in the middle of freaking nowhere, I thought, panicking.

Sporty coughed and wheezed and, after what felt like an eternity, finally expelled the hay. I hadn't realized just how long I was holding my breath until I exhaled in relief.

We walked a little while longer to make sure Sporty had recovered, but continued to look over our shoulders for the riders coming up behind us. We were sure they had made time on us. As we rode into the final vet check at around 90 miles, the horses had a shine to their eyes. It was now sunset, and once again, the headlamps went on. We hadn't been in the vet check for very long when the rider behind us arrived.

The moon started coming up as Pa and I hit the trail again for our final loop, casting shadows behind thousands of sagebrush shrubs and illuminating the course ahead of us. When the wind changed, we could feel dust enveloping us. We rode in the dark and only briefly switched on a light at a crossroad to identify which path to turn down, not wanting to alert the rider behind us of our location. A glance behind us revealed the rider's light, and we stepped up the pace for the last few miles.

We arrived back at camp only a few minutes ahead of the 3rd-place rider. My dad let me claim the win, even though we came in together. After un-tacking the horses and throwing a light fleece blanket over them, we headed to the vet for our final check. I asked my mom to bring Goober out for the final exam; my ankles were throbbing in pain. We had trotted for close to 85 of the 100 miles, with my ankles and calves serving as shock absorbers each time I came back down from a post, in rhythm to Goober's trot. Posting is when you come out of the saddle with each stride—it's pretty much like doing a squat. That's almost 100 miles of hybrid squats. No wonder I could barely walk.

Passing the final vet exam with ease, we returned to the trailer and I pulled off my crusty, dirt-covered socks to reveal my stiff and swollen ankles. My parents told me they would show Goober to the vet for the Best Condition judging in an hour. I climbed straight into my sleeping bag. After close to 13 exhausting hours in the saddle, sleep came quickly.

The following morning, I was delighted to learn that, on top of winning the race, Goober and I had also won the Best Condition award, which was presented to one of the top 10 horses that finished strongest. The vets rate your horse based on the factors listed on your vet card. For example, they are marked down for soreness, quiet gut sounds, and dehydration. Other factors, such as time and the weight of the rider and tack combined are taken into account. A horse with a heavier rider gets more points than a horse carrying a lighter person. This made the win even more impressive, that Goober's vet scores were high enough to make up for my light weight.

The drive home was full of excitement and chatter as we discussed the exhilarating experience of starting and finishing our ride in the dark. We had a great time showing off our rubs, wounds, chapped lips, and dirty fingernails. All of us were looking forward to a shower.

After that experience, Goober and I bonded, and he quickly worked his way into my heart. He liked the extra attention I showed him. My parents let me know I could continue piloting him for the next few rides. I dreamt of the places where we would go together, but they were still only dreams.

The next day at school, my ankles were still swollen. I smiled, thinking of the race and trying to hide my hobble as I walked between classes. For an exercise in Spanish class, the teacher asked us to briefly share what we had done over the weekend. While most of my classmates related average weekend activities—hanging out with friends, playing video games, or doing homework—I said, *"Yo monto mi caballo"* ("I rode my horse").

I didn't go into detail about the race or even mention it. Even in ninth grade, I was still known as the Horse-Crazy Girl, and it didn't matter if anyone knew about the excitement in my life outside of school. Our horse adventures were my little secret that I didn't share with many people. I never mentioned the exciting emails from the crown prince of Malaysia, who had sent scouts from South Africa to inspect our horses. My family's trip to the UAE was something I only brought up if someone asked about it. Maybe I wanted to be humble, or perhaps I thought my classmates wouldn't understand the scope of the horse world and my involvement in it.

My English teacher certainly knew about it, though. In my creative writing class, I wrote poems about my adventures with Goober, our race at the Oregon 100, the heartbreak of selling Focus, and other stories about the horses that came into our stables and left with a piece of my heart. Some of my stories may have bored my teacher. But even if he didn't read them, I still loved re-living the stories through my keyboard and creating new ones in the saddle.

CHAPTER 7

Moving Up to Varsity

After a horse completes a 100-mile race, their attitude changes. They may develop quite the head on their shoulders and feel invincible.

This was most certainly true for Goober. He started acting like pretty hot stuff, quickly growing up from the innocent baby that got away with everything to bossing horses around and bonding with the ladies. Goober now thought he was quite the stud.

After the 100-mile race and a long winter break, we began training the unruly seven-year-old for his third endurance season. I rode him again in the first race of the season, and it was nice to be riding a horse who could be competitive. Goober could absolutely fly with a fast extended trot. He would throw his feet in front of him—all four feet off the ground—and land with the momentum to drive us farther down the trail, eating up the miles. Although I wasn't planning on riding Goober at Tevis, I was training him alongside the horses we were planning to take.

To prepare our horses for Tevis, I spent a lot of time training on Gray Butte and Still Hill. Gray Butte is a little under a mile and a half, with an incline at about a 15 percent grade. It was our bread and butter for Tevis training. While hill training is great for getting a horse in shape, it can become routine and uninteresting. With the youngsters, we did it slowly and only once, but with our Tevis horses, we pushed them up at a steady pace and did it a couple of times.

Goober really impressed us on Gray Butte. I would push him up the hill, monitoring his heart rate. When we reached the top, he always found a little extra in the tank to make sure he "won" and was the first horse to the top of the hill. I would dismount and lead him off the hill in hand to preserve his legs; the downhills caused a lot more strain on the tendons. Walking off the hills, I would regularly check Goober's heart rate to see how fast he was recovering.

On one particular training ride, Goober gave us a glimpse at the champion he was. After peaking Gray Butte, we stopped the horses about a mile down the hill to measure their heart rates and let them graze on some of the range grass. My watch, which was synced to Goober's heart rate monitor, showed his pulse at 36 beats per minute. That number is incredibly low and impressive, especially after the elevation gain of going up the hill.

Goober's favorite workout—and mine, too—was doing sprints in the flats. One-mile fartleks, half out of control, standing in my stirrups the whole time, left my thighs stinging and my shoulders tight from holding Goober back. But we both loved it. Goober also loved head-to-head racing, looking the horse next to him in the eye and giving an extra burst of speed at the end. He had a lot of kick, and when I gave him just a little extra rein, he plunged forward as if downshifting. The power of Goober beneath me, running at top speeds, was exhilarating as we galloped down the lane.

Getting the horses ready for races, and especially for Tevis, we were in heavy training mode even when we really didn't feel like it. The dedication it takes to be one of the best and most successful endurance stables doesn't mean you train when you feel like it; it's the days you train when you don't feel like it that put you on top. I didn't have the luxury of being a fair-weather rider. If we had a training ride on the schedule, we were saddled up and trained. The only time we would adjust our schedule for the weather was if the next day was going to be hot. The hotter the better for our heat training. When most people were heading to the pool to cool down, we were loading up the horses for training. Even though the central Oregon heat has nothing on the heat in the canyons at Tevis, we did our best to prepare.

Walking off Still Hill, an incline that was much shorter and a little steeper than Gray Butte, sweat would drip off my face. The base of the hill consisted of a random sand pit. Occasionally, if we would lolly-gag through the sand pit with Goober, he would take the opportunity to roll in the sand, scratching his body dramatically, despite having his saddle on.

I didn't usually carry water bottles so I could train myself for the heat, too. A few hundred yards beyond the base of Still Hill are some water troughs, filled with water that comes straight out of the ground from some natural springs. The water is refreshingly cool, and after working the horses, they get to enjoy splashing around in it a little and rehydrating. Every once in a while, on an extra-hot day, Barrak and I would jump off our horses into the water tanks and cool off with them. Sometimes I would drink cool water straight out of the pipe that came from the ground.

"Well," Barrak would ask occasionally, "once we get the horses cooled off and washed down at home, should we hit the river?"

It was one of our favorite summer activities. We had a secret swimming hole in the Deschutes River that was hardly ever occupied and deep enough that I have never touched the bottom. Once we had cooled off at the swimming hole, we would walk downriver a bit to where it was shallower and catch some crawdads. There was nothing better than some crawdads with butter at the end of a long day of training.

Sometimes, when I regretted not bringing water on our extra-hot training rides, the reward of going swimming was the only thing that kept me going. That, and hoping someday I would win the Tevis Cup.

The training was paying off; our horses were racing well and making us proud. Goober was competing right alongside our veteran horses and won another Best Condition award in a 50-mile race. He also finished a more competitive and challenging 100-miler in the top 10.

After Goober's second 100-mile race, he once again found himself recovering on pasture. When the horses are on break, they love to show off by bucking and racing each other all over the open space. Unfortunately, we returned to the pasture to discover several cuts along the inside of Goober's front and hind legs. Although we hadn't planned on taking him to Tevis because he still seemed immature, his newest injuries helped us finalize that decision. We were signed up for Tevis in 2016 with four solid horses, but we rarely ended up riding the horses we signed up. In the last few weeks before Tevis, we are always shuffling horses and riders.

That year, at the final training race before Tevis, a broker contacted us. "I have some clients looking for top endurance horses," he said. "We are going to be at the race this weekend, scouting. Could we look at some of your horses?"

These are the kind of clients that have an expansive checkbook and can pick out pretty much any horse they want. They race horses internationally and have scouts in about every country, picking out the best horses and flying them to their royal stables in the Middle East. Their stable of horses is similar to a football team. These equine athletes are an investment, and are given excellent care with top-of-the-line equipment and research. The stables are continually refining the team and striving to bring out each horse's full potential. The broker assured us that this stable has a good reputation and took top care of their horses.

At the local race, the scout introduced us to her clients. The team consisted of several vets, a couple of riders who weighed next to nothing, and some trainers. The chilling June rain was soaking through the horse's fleece blankets as we hurried around, taking care of our vet check duties. We were trying to get everything taken care of in the limited hold time, but the scout and her clients were distracting us from what needed to be done to care for and prepare our horses.

The scout walked through the mountain meadow where the vets stopped the horses 30 miles into the race. "My clients like the looks of your chestnut gelding with all the white," the broker said. "They would be interested in buying him."

She was referring to the horse my mom was riding. We had named him BES Oregon Chrome—BES after Blakeley Endurance Stables, and Oregon Chrome after the famous thoroughbred racehorse, California Chrome. This horse of ours had phenomenally low heart rates and recovery times.

"Okay, well, we don't really want to sell Chrome," my dad said. "Gabriela has him signed up for Tevis."

"Think it over," the scout persisted. "Consider whether riding him at Tevis is more important than a sale. If you change your mind, let me know, and we will make this happen."

"We would probably sell him for something around a hundred grand," Pa replied, throwing out a ridiculously high price. Only big-name riders got that kind of price for their top horses.

The broker didn't even flinch at the exorbitant price. "Okay. Think about it and get back to me after the race," she said.

For the rest of the 50-mile ride, we talked about how crazy it would be to send Chrome overseas. Prominent people in the industry were beginning to take notice of us and our horses.

The freezing rain drove us home as soon as we crossed the finish line. The sooner we got the horses back to the barn, the faster they would recover. We didn't run into the potential buyers again in our haste to get home, but the broker had our number. We thought it was unlikely that they would pursue the sale.

During the hour-long drive home, we talked about the race and analyzed how to improve for the next one: Tevis.

"The horses did well today," I chimed in as I stretched my shoulders, painfully sore from holding my horse back for 50 miles. "I think they're ready for Tevis."

"Bummer it was so cold," Mom remarked. "We only have six more weeks until Tevis, and we didn't get much heat training this year."

"Our training has been going well," I said. "It just hasn't gotten that hot here yet. Hopefully it will be cooler than normal at Tevis, too. We can't compete against horses from Florida and California who've been training in the heat all year."

We grew quiet as we drove on. We were each thinking about what we needed to do in the next six weeks to maximize our last few training rides. It boiled down to a couple weeks of rest, followed by light regenerative rides the third week, and then hard training and peaking on the fourth week. After that, we would taper off and ease back. The last week consisted of just moving them enough so they wouldn't have an overflow of energy and get hurt while traveling and prepping.

"I just got a text from the broker," Mom said suddenly. "Her clients are leaving the race and want to come to look at our horses and make us a deal on Chrome." She looked up from her phone in disbelief. We all had thought they weren't that interested, especially after Pa had thrown out the crazy price.

We arrived home mid-afternoon and put the horses away

with some oats and thin blankets. The rain had quit as soon as we passed the foothills of the Cascades, and the sun was out. We scrambled around, unloading the gear from the horse trailer, and waited for the potential buyers to arrive.

They caravanned up our driveway and introduced the crew, eager to meet our horses. The first one they wanted to see was Chrome. They did a thorough examination and told their broker to consult us on a price. After a bit of negotiating, we settled for a much higher price than what we had ever sold a horse for; however, it was less than half of what we had asked for at the race. It was a contingent sale, depending on how well he did at the vet's examination.

We led Chrome to the garage, where we had electricity, and they pulled their x-ray and ultrasound machines out of the rental car. My family and I held our breath as the vet worked his way around Chrome, exploring every joint of his legs, the soft tissue, and the tendons below his knees. After taking multiple pictures of each joint from different angles, the vet from Spain gave us the okay and said everything was clear.

The buyers took photos and extensive notes on their new horse. They wanted to know what other horses we had, and after telling them about a few other choices, they followed us on a quick drive to my great-uncle's potato farm, where the rest of our herd was pastured. The group of shiny, well-muscled Arabian racehorses came cantering up to the trailer, since it always signaled grain.

The buyers hopped out of their rental cars and walked quickly over to the herd. "They are like kids in a candy store," the broker told my mom as she watched her clients examine our horses.

We showed them the gelding we had for sale, and their rider galloped him around the 10-acre pasture several times before dismounting with a big smile. The pair was half out of control and completely enjoying each other.

We set the horse aside for them and continued our walk through the herd. The vet put a halter on a young mare named Rumor and asked us about her. She had not raced yet and was only four years old, but she could run like nobody's business. The buyers really wanted her, but so did we. We had high hopes for Rumor, and they tried to convince us to sell her. However, they ended up looking at our more proven horses.

After attempting to buy several of our other horses that weren't FEI qualified, they asked about Goober. I really enjoyed racing Goober, and his cocky yet lazy personality was endearing. He was the herd clown and a real, honest-to-goodness goober, but also one of our most talented horses.

Though Goober was one of our best horses physically, he was a little frustrating to work with. He loved competition and racing fast, but training on trails and trotting for endless miles didn't require enough brain stimulation for him. He seemed like the kind of horse that would do well in the Middle East. He got easily bored training on single-track trails when he was just following other horses, and sometimes he needed a lot of encouragement. When he was in the lead, it was too much responsibility for him and he spooked a lot.

After a very brief trial ride, they made an offer on Goober. We contemplated back and forth, weighing the loss of Goober against the financial impact this sale would have for our family. It was an offer we couldn't decline, and we accepted it—the same terms and price as Chrome's sale.

We loaded Goober and the other gelding into the trailer and set off to our home for the x-ray examination. We brought out spotlights to guide the vets around the horses, started a bonfire for the rest of the crew to enjoy, and ordered a vegetarian pizza for our guests. It was a festive atmosphere, especially for my family; we knew the considerable financial impact these sales would have on our stable.

Goober was always a pill when things didn't go his way, and the vet administered an extra sedative to hold him still while they continued working. Halfway through the other gelding's third leg exam, they discovered a bone chip. The vets consulted with the crew, decided it was too risky to invest in the horse, and, sadly, put him back into the pen.

It was pretty late when the vets finally got around to Goober's final leg exam. Evidently the radiographs revealed a concerning image, but my family's untrained eyes couldn't make out where the concern lay. It seemed that Goober's OCD from when he was a yearling was still there, and it hadn't gotten any better. There was still the cyst in that stifle, which was the biggest concern from his original vet report. It could potentially lead to a severe injury in a critical location. Pretty much a deal breaker.

"He will be fine here, with the hills and speed you guys race in," the vet reported to us, "but with increased speed and sand, we aren't sure he will stay sound. He is a nice horse, but we will pass on buying him."

We enjoyed the pizza with our new acquaintances late into the evening, and then said our goodbyes. We would be in touch again once they finalized the deal for Chrome.

My family wasn't disappointed that Goober didn't sell. It would have been nice financially, but we were happy to keep him. We could enjoy him without ever regretting the decision. But we also had this worst-case scenario looming overhead. What we understood from the vet was that, if the cyst chipped off, it would float around in the stifle joint and cause some serious damage, potentially leading to a career-ending injury.

With my mom's Tevis mount sold, we once again had to redo our Tevis arrangements. I offered for her to ride Moondanzer, the horse I was signed up with. I told my parents I could ride Goober, but even though he was all healed from his pasture scrapes, I was a little worried about the results of the vet exam.

Pa pointed out that Goober and I had successfully completed two 100-mile races together, and that he had never shown any signs of lameness the whole time we had owned him. The vet had mostly been concerned about the speed and sand in Middle Eastern racing, and because it was such a huge investment for them, they didn't want to take even the slightest chance that he wouldn't be able to meet their expectations. My dad thought it would be fine to take Goober to Tevis, but he wanted to do it himself.

"I really wouldn't feel comfortable with you on Goober," Pa said. "He's still only seven, and the technical trail will require his full concentration. I would feel more comfortable with you on Sporty, and me on Goober." 451

He was looking forward to the challenge of taking Goober. I didn't argue, and gladly accepted the offer to take Sporty, a more surefooted, seasoned horse. Sporty had finished the Oregon 100 super strong with me and Goober, and he was a really powerful horse. He had completed 85 miles of Tevis the year before, and we predicted that he would easily be able to finish Tevis toward the front.

Sporty reminded me a lot of Taii Myr, the horse I rode on my first Tevis attempt. They had the same blaze and were both well-muscled and quick on their feet. Because Pa had been training Sporty, he was used to riding with a heavier load; with my light weight, if I rode him well, I could maybe even be a contender for top 10.

CHAPTER 8

Goober and Tevis?

It didn't take long to adjust to the last-minute change of plans. I got along well with Sporty and was bonding well with the cute chestnut gelding, despite constantly having to apply Desitin to his sunburned nose. I was confident that I would be running by his side at the Haggin Cup judging. Nine years after watching my first judging, I was ready to catch that dream, and work toward my biggest dream of all: winning Tevis.

The last week of preparation went by quickly, between the stress of packing for a week-long camping trip, adding an additional four horses, packing for their needs, and preparing for a point-to-point horse race. Mixing electrolytes, packing human and horse food, and preparing the tack and equipment left us with little time to relax.

Everybody had an important job. While my mom packed the tack and equipment, I started shaving the horses' hair around their large muscles to help with cooling. The guys were in charge of applying additional protection for the horses' feet, for the extra-rocky trail. We liked to pull the shoes off the horses a few days before applying the hoof protection in order to let their feet dry. We do this to ensure the glue sticks better and their feet are healthier.

While my mom and I were doing some pre-race shopping in town, we got a call from Barrak. "The horses are running down the road through the neighborhood," he exclaimed.

The Tevis Gremlins were hard at work. This was the second time the horses had escaped their pen a week before Tevis. The year before, the owner of the property where we had been pasturing them forgot to close the gate. The timing couldn't have been worse.

"What? How'd they get out?"

"Goober opened the gate at the end of the driveway." I could hear the irritation in Barrak's voice on speakerphone.

"Are you serious?" I asked in disbelief. "The heavy wooden one?"

"Yep, there are bite marks on the two-by-four that holds it shut."

"Oh, that stinker," Mom said. Of all times, Goober had to do this a week before Tevis, when the horses were barefoot. "Do you need help putting them back? We can be home in 20 minutes."

"We should be fine," Barrak replied. "I just really hope their feet didn't chip out too much on the asphalt."

Even though Goober was now signed up to take on the Tevis Cup, he still hadn't outgrown his rambunctious youth and was causing just as much trouble as before. The only difference was that, instead of harmless bucket-stealing, he was now potentially injuring one of our Tevis horses that we had worked all year to get ready for the important race. Thankfully, their feet weren't injured enough to prevent Barrak and Pa from being able to securely apply the hoof boots and they hadn't made it far enough up the road to encounter too much traffic.

After days of packing and preparing, we hit the open road. Long hauls are wearing on the horses, and we wanted them to arrive in

Truckee fresh and well-hydrated. So, we split the drive into two days, spending the night out in the desert outside Alturas, California, to give the horses a break from traveling before pushing through to base camp.

Arriving at the start of Tevis on a Thursday evening, the horses quickly settled into their makeshift corral. We had one full day on Friday to get everything ready before the race on Saturday. Goober was the only one in the group attempting Tevis for the first time. The most seasoned of the bunch, Emmers, had started four times but only finished half of his starts. Moondanzer also had a 50 percent completion rate, but only out of two starts. Sporty had yet to finish.

The day of the race, we got up at 3:00 AM. I don't drink coffee, but I knew that nerves and adrenaline would keep me going. After a brief warm-up, we headed to the start line. There was a lot of commotion, with horses hollering through the dark woods while competitors' headlamps illuminated blinding clouds of dust. We made our way down the road in silence and darkness, trying to project calmness for the horses to sense and absorb.

At Tevis, the competitors are divided into two fields. Based on the horses' past race records, the most competitive riders are placed in pen one. But even those who don't make it into pen one still try to place well.

We handed our tickets to the timers so we could enter pen one, and joined the 60 horses that were milling around. Some horses had green glow sticks taped to their breast collars, to illuminate the trail ahead of them with soft light. Others had red glow sticks attached to their tails to indicate that the horse would kick if you got too close. Besides the glow sticks and the light of the moon, there was complete darkness.

The ride managers opened up the road to allow the horses to make their way about half a mile to the official ride start. Tevis

has a different level of excitement than local races, and the horses can tell it's a big deal. My dad dismounted just in time to prevent Goober from side-stepping into another excited horse. It
was the biggest crowd he had ever been in, and Pa hand-walked
Goober for a while until he slowly began to settle down.

A large banner that read "Western States 100 – Start" indicat-
ed we had reached the point of no return. Racers waited tensely
for the moment when the clock would hit 5:15 am.

"Three minutes," the timers shouted over the sound of horses pawing and prancing. Several horses let out a loud snort, indi-
cating that they were ready and didn't enjoy having to wait.

The seconds ticked by, and even Sporty, a seasoned, well-
trained horse, became antsy. Horses were switching positions,
and riders wormed their way to the front of the group. My family
had secured a position close to the front of the group, maybe
around 15th or 20th place. Between the dust and the darkness, it
was hard to tell exactly how many horses were in front.

"One minute to go."

My heart echoed through my chest as I did a quick mental
check to make sure everything was ready, although it was too
late to change anything. Finally, my dad hopped on Goober and
turned him toward the trail. After a long, suspenseful minute, a
ride official called out: "Trail's open. See y'all in Auburn."

The extremely competitive riders shot down the trail. Sporty
and Goober fell into a gallop, and there was no convincing them
that they should trot on the dusty road. I was relieved to have a
bandana over my nose and mouth, but felt bad for the horse's
lungs.

The first several miles were a blur. We were still riding in
darkness and bumper to bumper with other horses through the
dark wooded forest. I gasped at the narrow trails and incredibly
steep drop-offs.

We emerged from the woods onto a dawn-lit bridge crossing the Truckee River below us. The sound of horses clopping across the asphalt echoed throughout the valley. Volunteers asked for rider numbers as horses trotted past. They needed to account for everyone and update the tracking webcast.

We crossed the bridge and cut straight up the bank, going past the historic Western States Trail marker and then back into the woods. Several switchbacks later, we reached the top of the hill and rode along the narrow trail parallel to Squaw Valley. Thick vegetation blocked the view of the ski lodge below.

I tensed as I heard the distinctive sound of plastic snap behind me. I spun around in my saddle and made eye contact with Pa, who was balancing on one stirrup.

"My stirrup broke," he stated grimly.

This was not the place for a tack malfunction. We've ridden thousands of miles in our stirrups, and they rarely ever break. We had checked all of our tack before the race, so a broken stirrup was one of the last things we expected. It happened right on a narrow trail with horses piling up behind us. Typical. Our only option was to keep moving forward. I managed to untie my light lead rope, and as the trail widened for a few feet, my dad was able to slip in front of me so I could hand it to him. He rode a little farther down the path with one stirrup while wrestling with the reins. He tied my rope in a loop around the front of his saddle to make a temporary foothold.

"Can you ask Bob and Cory to bring a spare stirrup to Robinson Flats?" Pa asked me.

Our crew consisted of Bob and Cory Davis and their friend, Gayle, from Chico, California. We had met them when they bought one of our horses, and we'd hit it off right away. They offered to crew for us at Tevis, and an extra hand is always appreciated. After spending time with them and getting to know the sweet couple better, we eventually gave them Taii Myr when we felt he should slow down from competitive racing. They were a perfect crew and always had what we needed at the vet stops, where they waited to assist us.

The first step in crewing at Tevis was to bring everything from Truckee to the finish in Auburn. Once our trailer was secured in Auburn, the crews made their way to the first vet checkpoint where crews were allowed, 36 miles into the race. Besides bringing all our gear to the vet checks, a crew helps with cooling the horses, having food and water laid out, and being there for moral support. The Davises were always calm and helped us not get too excited when we were in race mode.

The spare stirrup—the one thing we hadn't packed in the vet check bags—was in the trailer. I hoped they hadn't already dropped the trailer at the fairgrounds and were on their way to Robinson Flats.

"Not registered on networks" appeared on my cell phone's screen. *Of course*, I thought, *there's no cell reception out here.*

While jimmying around with the makeshift stirrup, we lost a bit of time on our other two family members. Goober started prancing sideways in his frustration at being slowed down. His hind feet landed on the edge of the trail, sending shale rock rolling down the hillside. I gasped, envisioning the scenario of Goober losing his balance.

Pa dropped the jacket he had been holding under his arm while trying to fix the stirrup. Hundreds of horses behind us trampled over it, leaving it a victim of the trail. Dormant ski lifts towering above the trail led my gaze to the top of the next hill. The next section of the course was visible and revealed a long double-lane climb where we could pull over.

"Can we come by?" asked the impatient riders behind us as the trail widened a touch. The trail was too narrow; there was no way the large group behind us could safely pass. It was only another quarter mile until the slim trail widened into a passable road. We sped up to accommodate the other riders.

The horses plowed up the road to Watson Monument. I finally found a spot with cell reception and left a brief message for our crew, hoping it would get through.

Thirteen miles into the race and about two-thirds of the way to the top of Watson Monument was another webcast station, accompanied by water troughs where we could hydrate the horses. Even though it was only 6:30 in the morning, the horses had already worked hard to climb up to these water tanks. Water already covered the plateau floor from the competitors in front of us cooling their horses.

After the challenging climb, our horses drank a lot. The brief stop was bustling with racers trying to get everything taken care of before heading off onto the narrow trail that led through the Granite Chief Wilderness. We caught back up to Barrak and my mom and agreed to ride together again for as long as possible. My dad held Sporty while I ran over to the volunteers and asked if anybody had a spare stirrup. I was disappointed but not surprised to be turned away empty-handed. Pa would have to keep riding in his makeshift stirrup.

We continued up the hefty climb, past the Olympic ski lodge and toward the peak of Watson Monument. Finally, as we reached the maximum elevation of 8,900 feet, I turned around in my saddle for one final glance at Squaw Valley. Lake Tahoe was shining bright blue, reflecting the early morning sun. I felt a smile creep onto my lips as the *Bonanza* theme played in my head and I envisioned the opening image of Lake Tahoe from the show I'd enjoyed watching as a kid.

We beat the sun as we descended into the shadowed, refreshingly cool Granite Chief Wilderness. Besides the traffic jam of horses, we had to deal with a technical trail of smooth granite boulders and mud from the fresh snowmelt. There were a few brief moments when I acknowledged my surroundings and gasped at the rugged beauty of the Sierra Mountains. The blooming sunflowers, green grass growing in the high country, and fresh mountain air made me want to build a little cabin right alongside the trail and spend forever right there. The cherry on top was enjoying the scene from the back of a horse and truly living in the moment.

Nineteen miles into the race is the first time a vet looks at a Tevis horse. It is a simple trot-by examination, and riders don't need to get off the horses unless the vet thinks they see something wrong. If the vet suspects a horse is off, they will call you back and take a closer look. With nine more examinations in the race, we didn't want to waste any time, and all of our horses felt good.

I ran to the volunteers, hoping again that there would be a spare stirrup or at least some duct tape. Unlike my last effort, this time I returned with a full-functioning stirrup. We took advantage of the few minutes it took for the horses to drink to do the stirrup swap. Before continuing down the trail, we rode past the veterinarians without losing any time. As we made our way to Lyons Ridge, my dad rode more comfortably balanced, now that he had two functioning stirrups. We rode past the photographers waiting to capture the iconic Tevis shot of horses conquering Cougar Rock before moving on to the next vet stop.

It can be overwhelming to think of completing 100 miles in a race. I prefer to look at it as one vet stop at a time; this makes it a lot easier to digest. The first official vet check, called Red Star Ridge, is at 28 miles. There, the horses needed to meet a pulse criteria of 60 beats a minute while the vets do their first thorough examination. There are a lot of metabolic pulls at the first stop. The congestion in these early miles of the race can be challenging and mentally wearing on horses, resulting in tie-ups and horses not reaching the pulse criteria.

Once the vets examined my horse, we were free to leave whenever we wanted, unlike many races with a minimum hold time. The lack of hold time makes it challenging, because riders are responsible for taking care of their horse and managing their own time. Your horse needs to eat and recover a little, but you can't control when the competition leaves. Each horse is different. Some need extra food early in the race, where others just waste time and energy trying to eat since all they want to do is run. If a rider spends more time at a check, they may have to go faster on the trail to make up the time, but at the same time their horse may have more energy from resting the extra five minutes. It is important to manage your time wisely and ride according to your horse's needs.

Leaving the Redstar Ridge vet check, the horses usually feel re-energized and enjoy the change of pace as the trail widens. The eight-mile stretch from Redstar Ridge to the first of two mandatory holds is always a fast section and one of the few where you can make good time. It is a gradual decline, but not enough to prevent you from changing the gait from a trot to a gallop.

The hour hold at Robinson Flats is the first place riders get to see their crew. An hour may seem like a long time, but it flew by as I cooled my horse down, presented him to the vet, made sure he ate and drank, and took a minute to feed myself. Then, after switching to a dry saddle pad and fresh leg boots for the horses, I refilled our electrolyte bottles and took a second to sit down and rest, and then it was time to leave again.

Our horses were doing well at this stop. They were not too worked up and were taking care of themselves by eating and drinking. Goober was acting like an old pro, settling down well into the race routine. We were happy he could keep up with our other three experienced horses, despite this being his first Tevis attempt.

We continued our race through several more vet stops and then plunged into the first of three dramatic canyons. Around noon, when the sun was beating down on the trail, hitting the canyons felt like running into a wall of heat, and the pace of the race changed. The main focus shifted slightly to racing the elements, conserving energy, and staying in the game, versus rallying for positions and beating the competition.

Every competitor had a different strategy for entering the canyons. Some made up their time there because they trained in the hills, while others were strong runners and hit the canyons cautiously on foot, leading their horses. We tried to conserve a reasonable amount of energy and hoped to have gas left in the tank for the remaining 36 miles after the last canyon. I had also been running at home to prepare for the canyons; I wanted to help my horse by running them on foot.

We began the descent into the endless abyss. Shrub oak and eucalyptus canopied and blocked the sun. Rather than provide relief from the late July heat beating down on me and Sporty, the trees stifled any fresh air and made the canyons uncomfortably hot and muggy. The only relief was in the breeze we created by moving.

"Should I get off here?" I asked Barrak, who knew the trail well. "It's starting to get steep."

"Give it a couple more switchbacks," he answered. "It levels out for a couple of switchbacks, and you'll be faster riding on Sporty than on foot."

Barrak was already on foot, almost putting Emmers into a gallop with the combined momentum of gravity pulling him forward and his legs propelling him down the hill.

I caught my breath a little, looking down the hillside and seeing several switchbacks below. The trees blocked most of the view and, thankfully, I couldn't see all the way to the river flowing through the ravine at the bottom of the canyon. I was anxious to get off my horse and continue on foot, trusting my own feet more at this point than my horse's. I could hear Goober scrambling over a few rocks. I turned in my saddle to see him trip a little, probably because he was dozing off without having his rider on him. My dad was on foot as well.

"You can get off here," my brother directed me.

I already had my lead rope untied. I swung over Sporty's neck, using the momentum to land in front of my horse and continue running down the switchback.

Switchback after switchback, we continued down that first canyon. About half a mile down, the footing leveled out a little bit, and Sporty was pushing me from behind, eager to go faster. I popped him in the nose with the end of my rope a couple of times, signaling him to slow down and give me more space. But he didn't get the memo.

"Wait, guys!" I screamed as Sporty's foot with its steel shoe scraped down my ankle. I hobbled a few steps, crimson liquid seeping into my sock, which was already gross and crusty from my lower legs rubbing against his flanks, absorbing his sweat. There was nothing besides my sock and my thin riding tights to protect my ankle from the impact of Sporty's hoof and shoe.

There was no way I could continue on foot, and this wasn't the place to stop because the trail was so narrow and the horses were impatient. Pa took off his ankle stabilizer (he rode with one due to an old injury) and slid it over my sock. I'm not sure if it was the heat, lack of food, or lack of sleep, but my pain tolerance was not high. I bit my bottom lip, swallowed some ibuprofen, and tried to fight back tears before remounting Sporty.

"It's a pretty bad injury." My dad looked at me sympathetically. "If you want to pull yourself once we get out of the canyon, that's totally fine."

I didn't like to quit, and I especially hated being pulled for something that was my fault. If my horse was hurt, I had no problem with it, but I didn't like to quit due to my own mistakes. But I felt reassured knowing that if it came down to it and I couldn't go on, I had Pa's blessing.

"Well, let's hope the ibuprofen kicks in before then." My words came out barely above a whisper.

My ankle throbbed as we continued trotting down the canyon. The downhill caused extra pressure from bracing against the stirrups. I forgot all about posture and locked my elbows, bracing with my arms against the pommel of the saddle and letting my left leg hang without much weight on it. I reflected on what I had done to get myself here and would not let this end my race prematurely. I had worked too hard for this.

By the time we reached the swinging bridge at the bottom of the canyon, my empty stomach had absorbed the ibuprofen, and the pain had eased up significantly. We clopped across the bridge, admiring the clear water rushing below us down the ravine. Halfway over, the bridge began to bounce. Sporty bolted and rear-ended Emmers ahead of us. Goober crowded us from behind. We traveled across the bridge as quickly as possible to get the nervous horses on solid footing again.

It was about a mile from the river, which was at a 2,800-foot elevation, up to the top of the canyon at 4,300 feet. It felt like the switchbacks would never end. When I thought we had reached the top, they just seemed to keep going. By then, the horses had begun feeling the strenuous effects of the climb, and once again, the race slowed down.

At the top of the canyon was a water stop called Devil's Thumb.

Under the shade of pine trees, cheerful volunteers handed out water, offered to fill water bottles with ice, and served watermelon and snacks. Although we were running in the top 15, the ground was already drenched from the riders ahead of us who had been cooling their horses and splashing water on the ground. Bucket after bucket was dumped onto the hot horses as they drank deep like camels. After they ate some hay, we continued on a refreshingly gradual incline to the vet stop one mile ahead.

We were coming into the abandoned mining town of Deadwood, and quitting wasn't an option for me. This was the vet stop where I had been pulled the year before. My ankle injury was now bearable, and Sporty was feeling strong. After the vet check, we rode past Deadwood, a small cemetery, and down into El Dorado Canyon. A mile and a half down, it is the longest of the three canyons. The trail led us down to 1,700 feet of elevation with 42 switchbacks to the bottom.

The seventh webcast station at Michigan Bluff was 1,800 feet above the El Dorado River. If I'd thought that first canyon was endless, this second one was even more deceivingly so.

They set up the refreshing water stop in the middle of the only street running through the small town of Michigan Bluff. The day the Tevis Cup is held, the town basically shuts down. Residents sit on their porches to watch the horses coming out of the second canyon. This is a spot where one can see endurance for what it really is—sweat, thirst, dirt, and hard work for both horses and riders.

The brief, refreshing stop at Michigan Bluff gave me a short break before continuing on to the Piper Junction Vet check. After vetting our horses, we reconvened around the water trough at Piper Junction to continue cooling them while letting them munch on some alfalfa and rest a bit.

"How'd everybody's horses do?" I asked, looking over

Sporty's vet card, which contained purely positive marks.

"Good," Barrak said. "How about you guys?" he asked my parents.

"Goober has to re-show," my dad said as he headed over to massage Goober. "He has a tight muscle from coming out of those canyons."

What if it's not the muscle, but the old injury the international buyers were worried about? I was always a worrier when it came to horse health. I tended to assume the worst.

Pa worked on loosening the muscle for a while, and Goober enjoyed the massage as he munched. We trotted him out again, but he didn't show much improvement. Pa had a half-hour to re-show Goober to the vet before getting pulled from the race.

"You guys go ahead," he said. "I'll keep working on Goober by stretching and massaging him. Hopefully we'll see you guys at Forest Hill."

Barrak, my mom, and I continued on the route for Auburn. We had little hope that we would see my dad and Goober ride into Forest Hill.

The last canyon between Piper Junction and Forest Hill was about half the length of the first two canyons. Red dirt and rocks over the trail made me feel like I was on another planet. The course wove through groves of mammoth manzanita bushes that were the same height as me on top of my horse. The smell of eucalyptus and scrub oak filled the late afternoon air. My lips were chapped and dry at this point. Even though I made it a point to hydrate, my water intake didn't equal the output of sweat.

Crossing Volcano Creek at the bottom of our last canyon, I could feel Sporty slip on the wet rocks coming out of the river. He seemed fine, and the climb from Volcano Creek to Forest Hill was more gradual than the other rises. Finally, the trail merged onto a paved thoroughfare leading into the town of Forest Hill.

When we hit the hard asphalt, I thought I felt Sporty making a shorter step with his left hind leg.

"Does Sporty look okay in the hind, or am I paranoid?" I asked my mom.

"He looks fine," she said reassuringly. "He's moving nicely, and his tail is centered. Don't worry about it."

There were spectators with garden hoses lining the street, allowing a narrow cooling channel for the contestants to ride through. Water drenched the road. It was a madhouse coming into this vet check.

The adrenaline kept me going as our crew stripped the saddle and other remaining tack off of Sporty. The horses enjoyed soaking up the cold water as their riders led them by hand through the crowd to where the pulse box was. The one-hour hold started once your horse's heart rate reached 64 beats per minute, so it was vital to have the volunteers measure your horse's heart rate as soon as possible so you could start your hold time.

An announcer called out rider numbers over the speakers as they emerged from the trail and about five minutes before they would arrive at the vet check, giving crews a couple of minutes to prepare for their arrival. Several competitors were close behind us, and now that the most demanding section of the race was over, we needed to focus again on making time and keeping an eye out for our competition.

We hit this bustling parking lot pitstop just before five o'clock in the afternoon. The California sun hadn't let up yet, and the refreshing stop, 68 miles into the race, gave riders and horses alike a mental and physical break during the hour-long hold. Water troughs and hay bales were scattered amongst the vendors, crews, spectators, taco trucks, massage tables, and vet examination lanes in the open area of the Forest Hill vet check.

In addition to the general duties performed at the vet stops, glow sticks were also taped to the horses' breast collars and headlamps secured to the riders' helmets. This was the last time crews were allowed to assist riders before the finish. Even winners and riders finishing in the top 10 still rode a bit in the dark.

We were waiting for our horse's heart rates to come down to 64 beats per minute, when "Number 170" came echoing through the staticky speakers.

"That's Pa's number," I said excitedly. "He must have worked through Goober's muscle cramp and they're on their way, heading up the road."

You can never give up hope until the vet actually pulls you. I knew my dad could take care of Goober, and I needed to just focus on my race and get Sporty through the vet check.

"Can you trot him out for me again?" the vet asked.

Trotting Sporty out for the vet, I was suddenly concerned because I knew he would never ask for a second trot out unless he thought he saw a problem. Sporty seemed fine to me, and I was sure we could work out whatever was going on. I came back and saw a grim look on the vet's face. He told me that Sporty was sore on his left hind leg. On closer examination of his lower limb, the vet noticed the difference between the red dirt sticking to his sweat and the dried blood.

It wasn't a deep cut. I figured he must have slipped on a rock crossing Volcano Creek. Sporty was sensitive and wouldn't let the vet touch his wound.

"Well, try to work him through it," the vet instructed me. "His muscles seem a little tight from compensating. Try massaging them and icing the cut. You have until the end of your hold for him to improve, or I have no choice but to pull him."

It is usually hard for a vet to tell riders that they can't continue; they understand how disappointing it is for the riders to fall short of their goal. Most riders take a pull with grace and

TOP: Baby Sanoma and Candy.

BOTTOM: Baby Barrak and Sanoma.

TOP: Sanoma and Candy.

BOTTOM: Baby Barrak and Sanoma on Candy.

TOP: Sanoma and Grandpa Buck horse logging.

BOTTOM: Sanoma and Victor.

TOP: Sanoma and Marathon at the Head Waters of the Rogue Endurance ride in southern Oregon, August 25, 2007.

BOTTOM: Sanoma and Flusi at the Prineville Ride 2008.

Weanling Goober, around 2009.

Weanling Goober, around 2009.

TOP: Sanoma and Midnite, summer 2011.

BOTTOM: Moondanzer, Sanoma on Midnite, and Barrak on Bugsy. This photo was taken in October 2011 in eastern Oregon.

TOP: Wasch on Taii Myr, Barrak on Bugsy, Gabriela on Hami, and Sanoma on Victor. May 19, 2012 at the Mt. Adams endurance ride in Washington State.

BOTTOM: Sanoma and Taii Myr at Elephants Truck, Tevis 2013. This photo was taken several minutes after witnessing the horse fall off of Cougar Rock.

TOP: Barrak and Emmers winning the Haggin Cup in 2014.

BOTTOM: Sanoma and Focus, late winter 2013.

TOP: Rashid and Focus racing in Abu Dhabi, November 21, 2014.

BOTTOM: Family photo at the Owyhee Canyonlands race in Idaho. Wasch on Moondanzer, Gabriela on Chromeo, Barrak on Pre, and Sanoma on Dreamchaser.

TOP: Barrak and Pre, Sanoma on Goober, and Wasch holding LeBron
and Chromeo on May 20, 2016, the day before the Mt. Adams endurance race
in Washington State.

BOTTOM:: Family photo from Tevis 2016. Gabriela on Moondanzer, Barrak on
Emmers, Wasch on Goober, and Sanoma on Sporty.

TOP: Wasch on Goober, Gabriela on Moondanzer, Barrak on Emmers, and Sanoma on Sporty passing through Michigan Bluff water stop at Tevis 2016.

BOTTOM: Nevada Derby Race-in, April 2, 2017. Sanoma and Goober racing in against Ann Marie Barnett on CA Zanes Dragonflyte, winning the 50 mile race in four hours and 35 minutes.

TOP: Sanoma and Luke, senior pictures April 1, 2018.

BOTTOM: Sanoma and Goober at the 2019 Tevis vet-in the day before the race.

TOP: Sanoma and Goober entering Robinson Flats vet check at mile 36 of the 2019 Tevis.

BOTTOM: Sanoma and Goober leaving Chicken Hawk at Tevis 2019.

TOP: Sanoma and Goober at Bottom of Bath Road, around mile 67 at Tevis 2019.

BOTTOM: Sanoma and Goober around mile 70 at Tevis 2019.

Sanoma and Goober and Jeremy and Etta at the finish line, Tevis 2019.

Sanoma and Goober at the Tevis 2019 Stadium finish.

Sanoma and Goober at the award ceremony the day after winning Tevis 2019.

TOP: Goober at the 2019 Haggin Cup judging, the morning after winning Tevis.

BOTTOM: Sanoma and Goober modeling for a saddle sponsorship, December 23, 2019.

Sanoma and Goober after Goober's sale, July 2020.

TOP AND BOTTOM: Sanoma and Goober after Goober's sale, July 2020.

TOP AND BOTTOM: Sanoma and Goober after Goober's sale, July 2020.

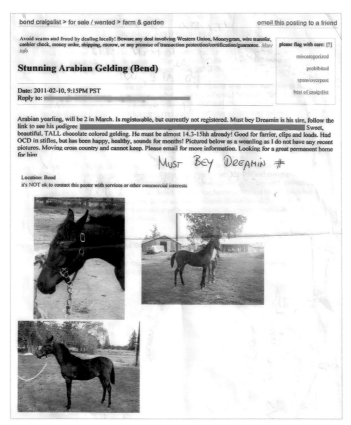

TOP: Goober's Craigslist ad.

BOTTOM: Goober back home in 2023.

are thankful for the extra care and caution given to their equine friends. But pulls still sting.

I hurried back to the spot our crew had set up for us and asked Cory to please round up some ice as I began massaging Sporty's muscle. After washing off the blood and dirt, it seemed that his lameness was coming from the muscle and not the small, superficial scrape as the vet had suggested. I paused to eat some watermelon myself. *So much for a break.*

My dad joined us and told us that Goober was doing better. Pa planned to slow down a bit and take it step by step, but he believed Goober could continue. Goober had passed the vet examination at Forest Hill with ease, so at least there was some good news.

"They are holding my vet card," I informed my dad. "Sporty is off on his hind."

Exhaustion, lack of sleep, hunger, stress, and everything combined made for weak emotions. I still hadn't been pulled, but it had been a long day. My ankle was sore, and my time was running out to get Sporty feeling better. I trotted him for Pa, and my hope slowly faded as Barrak and my mom started getting ready to head out on the trail again. I still had no confirmation that Sporty and I could continue. Even if I could get him through, I would be riding with my dad and Goober, and my chances of placing in the top 10 were out the window.

I was running out of time and had done all I could, but Sporty was still taking a shorter step with his left hind leg.

"Well, the good news is he is a little bit better but still not good enough for you to continue," the vet said sympathetically after watching Sporty trot out for the final time. "I'm going to have you head over to the treatment vets. They will examine him and make sure he is doing okay before hauling him back to the fairgrounds."

I was heartbroken. I was so close, yet so far from my goal. Sporty had been so strong. We were ready and we had done everything we could. Everything was perfect, except for that one rock he'd slipped on crossing the creek. Had it not been for his misstep . . . I would have given anything to have a time machine, to rewind an hour and a half and cross the creek more carefully.

I didn't want to accept our lot in this race, because it felt like that was going to be our year. But there was nothing I could do about it. In a ride of over 100 miles, there are a million things that can go wrong. That is also why Tevis is so addictive and challenging. I was discouraged by my back-to-back Tevis pulls, and as much as I wanted to try again the next year, I had mixed feelings about Tevis. I was in a love-hate relationship. Mostly hate, with just a little bit of love; the love of watching my family do well, while I couldn't seem to get it together.

Our crew tried to comfort me on the walk to the treatment vets. Liter bags of IV fluids hung suspended from ropes slung between a few trees. The site, wedged between an overgrown hedge and vet rigs, made for a nice, cool corner for the horses needing treatment. There was one lone horse who stood hooked up to the fluids. Vet wrap held the catheter in the horse's neck as he looked utterly defeated under the large pine trees. The horse had been pulled at a previous stop and then transported to Forest Hill to continue his treatment.

One of the treatment vets came over and put on her gloves to examine Sporty's cut. He wouldn't let her near it, and she got frustrated. She remembered him from the Robinson Flats vet check.

"This is the horse that wouldn't let us draw his blood at Robinson. Well, that is going to make it hard to sedate him to examine his cut and put in a catheter." She seemed generally in a bad mood.

"You don't need to do that. I can see it's not that bad of a cut. We've doctored way worse, and we have plenty of supplies at the trailer. He trusts me and will let me take care of it. Besides, why does he need a catheter?" I was getting a little frustrated myself. I knew why she wanted to put in a catheter. When you're not at a vet clinic, treatment gets really spendy.

"I know my horse, and he does not need IVs," I continued. "He's been drinking water all day. We got pulled for a sore back leg. Can you please just sign off so we can go to Auburn? He had straight A's on his vet card, and besides being a little sore, he is doing well and has a great attitude. I just want to get him back to the trailer and settled in so he can rest."

Reluctantly, she signed off and made arrangements for our transport to the fairgrounds.

I watched my dad and Goober head off down the trail into the evening just before Sporty and I got a ride to Auburn. My poor Sporty was a real trooper.

Because I got pulled, I had only the live webcast for updates on how the rest of the family was doing from here on out.

The section from Forest Hill to the next vet check at Francisco's is relatively straightforward. It's mostly downhill, and a large portion of the trail runs parallel to the American River. Depending on how fast they ride, competitors usually experience this stretch in the dark. The full moon reflects off the water and brightens the trail for the horses, who have excellent night vision. It is a beautiful and terrifying thing to trust your horse as you ride along narrow trails in the dark.

I was enormously relieved when I saw that my dad had arrived at Francisco's about an hour after Barrak and my mom left. Francisco's is the next vet stop after Forest Hill, with only 15 miles from there to the finish. It was dark and I held my breath, refreshing the browser every few minutes to make sure his status still said "on-course" and not "pulled."

The webcasting browser updated: Rider #170, Blakeley, Wasch – Checkpoint – Francisco's – OUT. I exhaled a sigh of relief, knowing there were only two more vet checks to get his completion. I continued to refresh the browser, and a little after 10:00 PM, Barrak and my mom arrived at Lower Quarry. They were running in the top 10 and had passed several riders on the stretch from Francisco's to Lower Quarry.

The hour without updates from any of my family members felt unusually long. I imagined all the worst-case scenarios, now that it was well into the night. I attempted to occupy myself by setting up camp and caring for Sporty to keep negative thoughts from creeping in and haunting my mind. I eventually headed to the finish line to watch the first few horses arrive.

The clear moon contrasted against the black night sky and illuminated the Auburn countryside of dry grass and hills. As I sat in the grass, my shoulders straightened a little when I noticed a change in my dad's ride status. He and Goober had arrived at Lower Quarry. I strained my memory to imagine the part of the trail they had just ridden between the two checks. The American River crossing is a breathtaking sight at night. The volunteers who take your number and update the live tracking feed are very friendly and are pretty much just partying and grilling along the riverbank. If you are a front runner, you traverse the river at dusk. The smell of the willows lining the river fills the air. The cold water comes up to about your knees when sitting on your horse and cools your sore, hot feet.

If you cross the river in the dark, glow sticks light up the border of the path, directing you where to cross. It feels like you're on a horse plane coming in for a landing on a lit-up runway. After crossing the river at 735 feet and riding a few miles farther, you arrive at the Lower Quarry vet check, six miles from the finish.

I quickly snapped back into reality at the sound of two horses emerging from the wooded trail and approaching the finish line. I could feel my heartbeat echoing through my chest. I couldn't quite make out the silhouettes of the two horses coming out of the woods. Based on their position when leaving Lower Quarry, it should have been Moon and Emmers with my mom and Barrak.

As the two horses approached the finish line and got closer to the banner lit up with twinkle lights that read "Congratulations," I could see that it was them. Bob, Cory, Gail, my grandma Alie, and I ran to the water trough to congratulate them. They had finished in 7th and 8th place and only had one final vet exam standing between them and their completion.

The final vet exam did not go well for Barrak. Emmers had a muscle cramp in his hind end. He had 40 minutes to re-show, and since my mom had received her completion, we all worked to get Emmer's muscle loosened up. We attempted everything we knew to loosen a cramp, even getting assistance from Garrett and Lisa Ford, fellow competitors who had already finished ahead of them. Garrett and Lisa were great fans of anything endurance-related—they had even sponsored Barrak in previous Tevis rides and were a huge source of support for my family. They knew about using essential minerals and new stretching techniques to loosen a cramp.

Under the time pressure, our optimism faded as he got worse with each trot out. Finally, Barrak accepted his reality as he re-showed Emmers to the vet under the large spotlights in McCain Stadium's center. I couldn't imagine the heartbreak he must have felt after riding 100 miles and not getting the credit because his horse had a tight muscle. I could see him fighting back tears. The emotion and adrenaline coupled with exhaustion and disappointment could bring anyone to tears.

After the long haul across the Sierras, the horses settled into the corral and joined Sporty for some rest. Then we headed back to the finish line to await my dad's arrival.

Fifty-two minutes into Sunday morning, Pa and Goober crossed the finish line in 16th place. Again, Goober vetted through with excellent scores. Even though he was tuckered out and looked like he had just run 100 miles, he had done well. I was incredibly proud of him; I had thought his race was over at Piper Junction.

An hour after finishing, the vets asked the riders to re-show their horses to make sure they were okay, so my mom and I took Goober back. He was upset to leave the friends he had just been reunited with and threw a little fit at the vet's, striking at the air and calling for his friends. He recovered well, and we joked with my dad that he could have probably gone a little faster based on the amount of energy behind Goober's tantrum, but we were proud of him either way. Even though Tevis had chewed us up and spat me and Barrak out without a completion, we were still happy with the outcome. Tevis has an average completion rate of 50 percent, so it was predictable that a couple of us wouldn't finish.

At the end of the day, it was a successful race for our family, and we were extra proud of our baby Goober who was all grown up and now a Tevis horse.

CHAPTER 9

Goober's Tevis Success

After Tevis in 2016, the herd dynamics made a 180-degree turn. We needed to downsize and re-homed quite a few of our horses, which gave us time to concentrate on our next string of future champions.

It is always exciting to see what a new horse has to offer. Some came from behind and surprised us with results we did not expect. Others plateaued and fell short. Our junior varsity of several talented and promising seven-year-olds was beginning to fill the varsity shoes. We cut the herd, retiring our older varsity to offer the up-and-comers our full attention. A new chapter had begun.

We retired Emmers back to his breeders, where they would appreciate him and he could enjoy a slower-paced life after racing. The woman who had bred Sporty wanted to buy him back, and despite my fondness for my buddy, we knew he would have a safe home there for the rest of his life.

Once the herd alphas were retired, the four horses that took over as the varsity were Goober, Quicksan, Pyro, and Luke. Goober stepped up as the boss. He was cocky and made sure to let the other horses know he was highest on the ladder. It was impressive that Goober had finished Tevis, but he was still only seven years old. Goober had the potential to be a champion. I liked his attitude and his sassy streak, even though it drove us crazy at times; it revealed his strong character and personality. After Tevis, my dad claimed Goober as his own. It was nice to see my dad riding a horse he enjoyed, and as long as Goober was still part of our herd, it didn't matter much to me who rode him.

Luke and Pyro were an excellent match that we had picked up the previous winter out of Utah. They were both seven-year-olds and tall, handsome boys. Pyro and I had completed a 100-mile race in his first race season, and we were all optimistic about his future. Although we got along well and I rode him during his first season, he connected better with my mom. Luke was a little more challenging than our other horses but showed just as much promise. He was beautiful and prancy. I liked hot, racy horses, so I didn't mind his jigging.

We got Quicksan when she was almost three years old. She was a well-bred mare, but we had our work with her cut out for us. We got her for free from her breeders, Dennis and Linda Tribby, because she had run through a gate and cut her legs up. These breeders were older and unable to catch the spirited three-year-old to doctor her. Finally, they told us that if we could catch her, we could have her. After five hours of chasing her around the ranch, my parents finally herded her into the horse trailer. It took a long time to earn her trust, but eventually, she was ready to start her training under saddle as a four-year-old.

Mom was training Quicksan to ride; she was a good girl but had a free spirit and a strong independent streak. She was doing well and making steady progress, and my mom felt confident enough to take her on her first few trail rides. On her seventh trail ride, Quicksan's free spirit got the better of her, and she didn't want to be told what to do. We were riding home from a few-mile trail ride, and she wanted to rush back to the trailer. My mom told her we had to slow down, and she responded by surprising Mom and bucking her off. My mom had to walk the mile and a half back to the trailer with a severely dislocated elbow.

After Quicksan showed her talent as a bucker, Barrak was the only one brave enough to ride her for a while. None of the rest of us fought him on it, and she became Barrak's horse.

The 2017 ride season started off rough, when we had an unusually wet winter and received close to thirty inches of snow. My family and I had finally saved enough air miles to buy some plane tickets and visit my family in Germany again. While we were gone, Oregon received a severe snowstorm and we returned home to find several horses injured after escaping from their pasture during the storm. They got tangled up and cut by some farm machinery hidden under the snowfall. Thankfully, we got home only a few days after the snowstorm, and the cold weather slowed any infection in their wounds. Goober's cuts weren't particularly deep, but they left some scars.

While Luke was healing from some of the cuts he had received on pasture, I took on the project of making another seven-year-old, Splash, my next champion. I had big dreams for Splash. The only thing going for him, my "ugly duckling," was his heart. Not his actual heart (which wasn't in the best shape), but his drive and bite. What he lacked in talent, looks, and ability, he made up for in his heart and head, and through hard work, time, and training, I would give him the rest and make him into a champion. Mentally he was a fighter and liked to push himself, and I was excited to see what we could accomplish together. I made out a plan and knew that someday I would have enough trust in Splash to take him to Tevis.

The sassy, strong-minded horse we had regretted buying at first was working his way into our hearts. When we purchased Splash, the sellers did not disclose that he was a windsucker. He had picked up this habit when he lived in one of the wealthiest communities in California. Windsucking is when a horse opens its mouth, bites into an object like a fence rail, and gulps air out of sheer boredom. It's an unhealthy habit that wears down a horse's incisors and can predispose him to colic and stomach ulcers.

We bought Splash sight unseen, and not only was the wind-sucking undisclosed, but he was a lot shorter than advertised. After having him brought up from Los Angeles, we wanted to resell him. We, of course, disclosed his windsucking and then could not find anybody who wanted to buy him, even at a greatly reduced price. He didn't fit in with our herd because he was shorter, not as talented, and not as good-looking as the rest, but I learned to love him. He was following my training plan, and I was playing the long game with him. I had loose plans to take him to Tevis in 2017, just to give him a feel for the course. Then, in 2018, I would try to top 10 with him, and 2019 would be our year to win.

I was excited to finally have a horse I would be able to give my full attention to and work hard with to reach my goal. Since we couldn't sell him and he wasn't worth much, I could invest all my heart into him, without the fear of having to sell him. I probably could have found a more talented horse to work with, but Splash was one of a kind and I enjoyed spending time with him. It didn't feel like work conditioning him, and more than that, I wanted to prove to everyone who hadn't given him a chance that he could be a champion someday.

The horses were shedding their winter coats, and the cold nights left them chilled in the late spring. Summer was just around the corner. Finishing up our chores, we headed into the house to get ready for the early start planned for the following day. We had an important, non-reschedulable appointment we had made months before on the more populated side of the mountains.

We woke up before the sun to get ready for the long drive, and my mom headed to the barn to take care of chores. As she walked to the horse's corral, all the horses came up to meet her at the gate. Shining her headlamp inside, she noticed that Splash was missing.

Mom made her way to the barn where Splash liked to hang out and found him wedged in the corner of the alleyway, lying down. It looked like a nice nap spot, but as she got closer, her headlamp shone on his sweat-drenched neck. It was a chilly morning, and my mom instantly got a knot in her stomach, knowing this wasn't normal. Taking him by the halter, she noticed a little blood on the walls. On closer examination, she discovered blood in his nose. When he didn't attempt to get up, my mom ran up the driveway to get help.

"Help!" she yelled. "It's Splash. He's sick!"

My dad cursed, which is something he seldom did. For Pa, cursing was a sign of how serious the situation was. He threw on some boots and a jacket and dashed to the barn. I was still in my pajamas, but I pulled my boots over my bare feet, slipped into my coat, and quickly followed my dad to the barn. Mom stopped in the garage on the way to grab a fleece blanket and some Banamine, an anti-inflammatory pain medication for horses.

"Come on, boy, get up," my dad coaxed. Splash tried, but he was wedged tightly between the two stalls and couldn't get his feet out in front of him. He was exhausted from struggling with the trap he had created in the barn aisle. My dad grabbed a firm hold on the top of Splash's withers and, with all his might, rolled him over onto his side. Now in front of the open stall, he was able to stretch his front legs out. Practically picking up the 900-pound horse, Pa finally got Splash to stand. We quickly covered him with a sweat-absorbing fleece blanket.

We led Splash out of the barn and continued to walk him around.

"Get some water and mix honey in it," my dad instructed me.

Running to the house to fetch some warm water, I was more optimistic now that Splash was on his feet. Returning with the water, I got a weird feeling when I saw my dad's eyes and those of the other horses reflected by my lamp's light. Splash's eyes looked hollow and lifeless. The sick horse stuck his nose into the water bucket and drank. Tragically, he didn't have enough energy to pick his head back up out of the bucket. His head remained submerged in the water, resting on the bottom of the bucket.

As we walked Splash around the garage and offered him water, he seemed completely out of it. It was as if zombies had taken over him, and he just kept walking. If we hadn't navigated, he would have plodded right into the side of the garage.

"Well, you guys better get going," my dad told us. "I'll do everything I can for Splash." He knew we had the important appointment to get to. Part of me wanted to stay and help, but there was nothing more I could do for Splash.

The three-hour drive over the Cascade Mountains was a grim one. My mom called my dad whenever we had cell service, and learned that Splash hadn't gotten any worse, but he also wasn't getting better. If there was anything we could do for Splash, I knew my dad would do it. The little horse was in the best hands possible.

"Try not to worry about it," my mom reassured me.

As soon as our appointment was over, we headed straight for the car. Besides being anxious to get home, the typical blustery western Oregon weather hurried us along. Once we left the city, we got on the freeway and headed home.

"Can we call Pa about Splash?" I asked my mom from the

passenger's seat.

She was looking straight at the road through the moderately paced windshield wipers as she replied, "It's already over."

I bit my bottom lip and knew what that meant. I had feared that possibility but hadn't let my mind go there. My stomach felt hollow, and my mouth was dry. We'd sold many horses that I'd never seen again, but losing one like this ... I couldn't keep from crying.

Our drive over the mountain was quiet. I laid my forehead against the window and watched the rain fall as we traveled the winding pass road running parallel to the McKenzie River. Tears were streaming down my face. It was like a scene from a sad movie, but tragically, it was my reality.

We arrived home as the sun set. My dad was a mess; I'd never seen him so down before. It was harder on him because he was there with Splash as he passed away.

We all hugged, and the ultimate question lingered in our minds: Why? What had happened to Splash? Not several hours earlier, he had nickered by the gate for his grain—and now he was awaiting placement into his grave?

"He was such a fighter," my dad said. "I know why you guys loved him."

My waterworks overflowed again. Just the thought of Splash brought a flood of tears. I had a flashback to that cold and rainy January night when my brother and dad picked Splash up in Los Angeles. They put Splash next to the car in the garage when they got home because the barn was full of hay. It was raining cats and dogs, and he was shivering from the drastic drop in temperature.

Splash had lived a life as a failed show horse before coming to us. He was always the underdog. I still had the dent in my ribs where he kicked me when I was giving my nine-year-old friend riding lessons. I thought of his unlikely friendship with Zeke, another horse we had bought on that trip to L.A. Now all we had left of Splash were memories.

"So what happened?" I asked. "Why did he die?"

"It was a brain injury," my dad said quietly. "He'd cut up the top of his head pretty good and hit it against the wall. He was trying to get momentum to stand up after he wedged himself into the corner, and he couldn't get his feet in front of him."

"For being such big, strong animals, horses sure are fragile," I said.

"They are," Pa agreed. "He fought to live, and even though there was nothing we could have done for him, he didn't give up until the very end."

Splash was the third horse I ever cried over. I didn't want to let him go.

A few weeks after losing Splash, I was still shaken up when my family decided to drive to Nevada again for the annual Nevada Derby. With only a handful of days left before the race, I was running across the lawn to bring my dad something when I heard a loud snap in my ankle. I feared the worst. It began swelling rapidly and was already starting to bruise.

My ankles were weak from a couple of past injuries, and even though the lawn was level and there was nothing to stumble over, my foot had rolled to the side. I assumed it was a bad sprain. I spent the afternoon in the emergency room, and the doctor confirmed my fears. He gave me a strong brace to support my ankle and told me to stay off it for a while.

Horse people are notorious for disobeying their doctor's orders, and I wasn't going to let this stand in the way of another race. Ibuprofen is a good friend of mine, and my dad had offered for me to ride my even better friend Goober in the race. No way was I going to miss out.

We had two fantastic days racing at the Nevada Derby. There was quite an elevation change through the Washoe Mountains, and we enjoyed some intense competition. We rode through herds of wild horses. Following a successful first day of reaching the top 10 in the 50-mile race, my mom and I saddled up Goober and Pyro, ready to hit the trail for another day of racing. The two boys traveled well together, and we started the race comfortably. The horses felt stronger the second day; we knew we didn't have to save them for another day of racing and could push them harder, consistently working our way to the front.

It was after 95 miles over two consecutive race days that, for the first time, I was able to race someone full out for the win. This sprint in finish showed me just what an incredible horse Goober really was. Leaving our final mandatory hold in 1st place, my mom and I put Pyro and Goober into a comfortable gallop and tried to gain some distance ahead of the horse that had left a minute after us. The remaining distance consisted of a flat and sandy loop. We could see every section of the track, with no trees to block the line of sight.

The other horse and rider, who were on their first day of racing, quickly made up the time difference and passed us. Though ahead of us, they were not pulling away. Horses have an easier time trying to catch another horse in front of them than they do keeping a lead. We didn't mind following, as long as we were within striking distance.

The trail loop made a 90-degree turn, pointing the horses back to the trailer. Goober was not ready to let go of the horse in front of us and pulled on the reins stronger than ever.

With about a mile to go, I asked my mom, "Should we go

catch her? She's speeding up." Goober was chomping at the bit (actually, he was pulling on his hackamore bridle, which is bit-less) so I knew what he was thinking.

"Wait a bit," Mom replied. "Once you're past her, you'll have to keep up a running pace. As long as you are behind her horse, Goober will be motivated to catch up."

We were galloping faster and faster to ensure that the horse didn't get too much of a lead on us.

"How about I let Goober go now?" I shouted. "I can see the finish line."

"Just a bit longer. Wait till we're around that corner ahead, then it's a straight shot to the finish line."

About half a mile later, with the finish clearly in view, I gave Goober his head and let him run. He was ready and surged forward. Like a horse charging into battle, his stride lengthened and his ears went back, showing his determination. Entirely focused, we quickly closed the gap on the leading horse.

I had never opened up a horse like that before. Our accelerating speed sucked the water from my eyes as we flew past the leading horse. I felt like I was flooring the gas on a sports car that shot up to 6,000 RPMs and sucked me into the seat. Not giving up that quickly, the horse we were racing kicked it up a notch, too. We sped along together, neck and neck as our horses galloped down the racecourse, dividing the sagebrush-filled prairie and kicking dust into the air behind them. Each fought hard for the lead, but when Goober put his mind to something, he could bite down and get it done.

Although I didn't need to, I kept pushing Goober on, standing in my stirrups and yelling, urging him to keep fighting. It was exhilarating when we flew past the finish line, a neck ahead of the other horse and rider.

"Easy boy!" I tried to rein Goober back as the vet check area loomed ahead, but he was having such a great time that he continued to sprint. I couldn't slow him down.

"Goober, stop!" I commanded, standing straighter in my stirrups to brace against his hackamore. It took us a while to decelerate before I could ease him back into a trot. Eventually, we came to a stop.

What a rush! These were the exhilarating moments I trained for.

Although the year had started off rough with the loss of Splash and injuries suffered by both Goober and Luke, we still had some good races. After our sprint for the win at the Nevada Derby, things just kept getting better and Goober and Pyro made us proud. Barrak and I crewed for my parents at Tevis and they finished in 5th and 6th place. I was so proud of my baby Goober on his second successful Tevis finish. He and my dad finished alongside my mom and Pyro. It was the first time Pyro had attempted Tevis, and Goober's first time placing in the top 10. After that successful race, we minded Goober's cockiness a little less, and the rest of the season went well.

Getting ready for Tevis began way before we actually started conditioning the horses in January. During the cold winter evenings, my family would stay up late into the night, sitting by the crackling fire in our log home and looking over Tevis statistics. We would create spreadsheets to compare our training over the years, analyzing the years we had done well and how we had trained that year.

We would also reminisce about the horses we had owned, and talk excitedly about the horses we were now bringing along. Each family member contributed to the conversations over popcorn and cups of cocoa. We all had theories about how to improve our training, and even if they didn't end up panning out, it was always fun to think about how to better our horses' training and nutritional routine.

The 2018 race season started off textbook-perfect. Our races went exactly as planned, and the horses were doing well. My family was beginning to get a reputation for consistently placing horses in the top 10 at Tevis, and we had a bit of a target on our backs going into the race. Since Pyro and Goober had finished 5th and 6th the year before, we had some expectations to meet.

I had put so much heart and energy into getting Splash ready for Tevis, and I wasn't quite ready to move onto my next horse. Luke was physically ready, but I wasn't comfortable riding him in the race. Instead, I filled the role of "crew boss." We recruited our friends as the biggest, most effective crew we'd ever had. There were eight of us in total, and we each wore T-shirts that read "Blakely Endurance Stables – Tevis Crew." I had a custom T-shirt made with "Boss" on it, in case anybody questioned my authority.

My dad had met one of our crew members, Rick, while doing disaster relief work in Puerto Rico from Hurricane Maria. Pa had invited him and his wife, Kim, to be part of our Tevis crew, and they flew out from Tennessee for the event. We also recruited Brian and Andrea, some good friends of ours from the west side of Oregon, to crew for us, as well as Josh, April, and Carmen from various parts of California.

We had the race planned to perfection, with the times figured to the minute. Barrak would be riding Quicksan at Tevis for the first time. Although it was her first attempt, she had already proven herself in other races, finishing a 100-miler faster than any of our horses ever had. My dad was riding Goober for the third time, and my mom was on Pyro for the second time. Since

I had ridden all three of the horses in 100-mile races, I made the perfect crew head.

I may have taken my role of boss a little too seriously. I mastered the art of delegating and had our crew running all over the place, getting water and ice to cool the horses, packing horse and human food for our crew stops, and helping take care of the racers during their vet checks. After we sent our riders back onto the trail at Forest Hill, our crew made its way back to the fairground, stopping for a brief dinner at the In-N-Out Burger in Auburn. While waiting for our orders, we were able to refresh the Tevis live webcast. It was hard to contain our excitement as we learned that my parents had made a few places and left Francisco's vet check in 2nd and 3rd place, with Barrak close behind in 5th place and only another 15 miles to go.

They held those positions to the finish, and my parents took 2nd and 3rd to Heather Reynolds. Both Heather and her husband Jeremy are extraordinary equestrians. They don't like to lose, and it is a rarity I've hardly ever seen. They are competitors you don't necessarily push your horse against, because your chances of beating them to the finish are slim. So, even when the opportunity to race for the win presented itself at the last vet check with 6 miles to go, my parents chose to come in with strong, healthy horses rather than push to beat Heather.

The next day at the Haggin Cup showing, my parents' decision paid off. Despite not winning the award, our horses were some of the freshest at the showing. Afterwards, Jeremy Reynolds came by and complimented our horses and the three top 5 plaques hanging on our trailer, mentioning that he didn't know of any other stable that had put three horses in the top 5. Coming from a top endurance rider, Jeremy's comments meant a lot to us.

Western States Trail Ride – Tevis Cup 100 Miles One Day
CHECKPOINT INFORMATION

Checkpoint	Mileage	From Robie	To Auburn	Check Type	Crew	Pulse	Cut-Off Times	Cut-Off Guidelines
Robie Park	0.0	0.0	100.0	Ride Start at 5:15 am	Yes		5:30 am OUT	
Squaw High Camp	13.0	13.0	87.0	Water Only (Vet Available)	NO			7:45 am IN
Lyon Ridge	8.5	21.5	78.5	Trot-By (Vet Available)	NO			9:00 am IN
Red Star Ridge	7.0	28.5	71.5	Gate & Go ++	NO	60		10:00 am IN
Robinson Flat	7.5	36.0	64.0	Gate to Hold: 1 Hr.	Yes (1)	60	12:30 pm PULSE 1:30 pm OUT	11:00 am IN
Dusty Corners	9.0	45.0	55.0	Water Only (No Check)	Ok (2)			
Last Chance	5.0	50.0	50.0	Gate & Go ++	NO	64	3:15 pm IN	3:00 pm IN
Devil's Thumb	4.0	54.0	46.0	Water only (No Check)	NO			
Deadwood	1.0	55.0	45.0	Gate & Go ++	NO	64	5:00 pm IN	4:30 pm IN
Michigan Bluff	7.5	62.5	37.5	Water Only (No Check)	Yes (3)			6:15 pm IN
Chicken Hawk	1.5	64.0	36.0	Gate and Go ++	Yes (4)	64		7:30 pm IN
Foresthill	4.0	68.0	32.0	Gate to Hold: 1 Hr.	Yes	64	8:45 pm PULSE 9:45 pm OUT	6:00 pm IN
Cal 2	10.0	78.0	22.0	Hay & Water (No Check)	NO		11:45 pm IN	
Francisco's	7.0	85.0	15.0	Gate & Go ++	NO	64	1:45 am IN	1:00 am IN
River Crossing	3.0	88.0	12.0	(No Check)	NO			
Lower Quarry	6.0	94.0	6.0	Gate & Go ++	NO	64	3:45 am IN 4:00 am Out	3:30 am IN
No Hands Bridge	2.0	96.0	4.0	(No Check)	Ok (2)			
Auburn Staging Area	4.0	100.0	0.0	Timed Finish	Yes (5)		5:15 am	40 minutes to reach pulse at McCann
McCann Stadium	0.1	100.1		"Fit to Continue" Vet Release Examination (6)	Yes	64 / Sound		

"Gate" = when criteria reached, present horse. Criteria must be met within 30 min. of arrival ++ After cut-off, Riders must leave 10 min. after vetting (1) Limit of one vehicle per rider with vehicle pass required and 2 crew members with wristband required. (2) Crews allowed, but not recommended. (3) Park short of Chicken Hawk Road and walk down to Michigan. (4) Walk in from Chicken Hawk Road. (5) Meet and walk with rider. (6) This mandatory vet exam, between 1 & 2 hours after McCann finish, does not affect finish status; vets want to assure themselves that all horses are okay. Haggin Cup exams are held on Sunday at 10:00 am–All First Ten Horses MUST remain at the Fairgrounds (See Rule 11) 4/12/2022

Tevis Cup checkpoint card.

CHAPTER 10

A Bad Start to the Year

After placing three horses in the top 5 at Tevis, the 2019 season felt like it was going to be our stable's year. Pyro, Quicksan, Luke, and Goober were becoming an unstoppable team. If the horses continued to train in mid-August like they had been training in mid-February, we had high hopes for them. But a lot can happen in six months—the Tevis gremlins, for instance.

Tevis gremlins are unfortunate things that only happen when preparing for or riding in Tevis. For example, my dad's stirrup breaking, and the likelihood of this happening on Tevis out of the thousands of miles we normally rode. And what are the odds that our horses would run down the road, barefoot, a week before Tevis? They hardly ever got out of their pens!

Over the last few years, we had fine-tuned our Tevis training to be as efficient as possible while putting the least amount of stress on our horses. We had the same three pre-Tevis races that we used as training: a 75-mile race at the local Still Prineville ride, a 50-mile race at Creek to Peak in Washington, and another 50-mile race at Bandit Springs, scheduled about six weeks before Tevis.

Luke had healed from his tendon injury, and I was now able to train him along with the other three big guns. Despite not having Tevis goals for Luke, we were having a blast pushing him to new limits.

May rolled around before we knew it, and we started getting ready for our first race. The horse-and-rider teams for the 75-mile race were the same as the previous year's Tevis combination: Pa on Goober, Mom on Pyro, and Barrak on Quicksan. I chose to ride the 50-mile distance race with Mickey, a gelding from our junior varsity that I thoroughly enjoyed riding. He was much calmer than Luke.

Since Mickey and I had won our shorter 50-mile race and were done earlier than the rest of the family on their 75-mile race, I stepped up to crew for them again. With another third of their race to go, Barrak and my mom came into the 50-mile vet check without my dad.

"Where's Pa?" I asked, alarmed.

"Pyro and Quicksan were feeling stronger, so we sped up a little," Mom said. "He should be in fairly soon."

Not long after they had vetted the horses through, Goober and my dad came in with my dad on foot. They went straight to the pulsers and, of course, Goober's heart rate had already reached the criteria. Not wasting any time, the vet examined Goober. He was doing fine, but he seemed to be having an off race. He was in the same shape as Pyro and Quicksan, but just wasn't quite as strong.

At the completion check after 75 miles, the vet noticed that Goober was a little stiff. Finish line pulls are the worst, but if your horse isn't fit to continue, they don't have any other option. We were happy that the stiffness was minimal enough to let him pass with lower grades on his final exam. The vet mentioned that Goober was sore, but 75 miles can cause soreness, and she wasn't concerned.

A few days after the race, Goober was just fine. We brushed off his stiffness as an electrolyte deficiency because later, we realized that we had mistakenly given him straight molasses during the race rather than electrolytes mixed with molasses. We'd mixed up the bottles while packing for the trip. It was a dumb mistake, and now we made sure to always taste the black liquid ourselves before administering it to the horses. That mixup, combined with his excessive sweating from the extra-warm spring day, must have contributed to Goober's soreness.

Shortly after the Prineville race, Barrak left for a vacation to Mongolia for about a month. I stayed home, training Quicksan for Barrak to ride at Tevis. Every photo my brother sent—wild horses, riding camels, sitting in yurts—made me regret not going with him.

In the meantime, we had some more serious horse inquiries. We received an offer for Pyro from the Royal Endurance Stables of Bahrain for a six-digit amount. My mom loved Pyro and this was a very hard decision to make. The stable would send one of its vets to examine Pyro and, upon the vet's approval, would proceed with the sale.

To prepare for the vet exam, Pyro needed new shoes. Having attended the well-known Pacific Coast Farrier School several years prior, Barrak usually handled all of our horses' hoof needs. Since he was out of town, we hired another farrier to reshoe Pyro, and unfortunately, the horse became lame from the farrier's shoeing ineptitude. Despite everything we were doing to help him feel better for the exam, Pyro wasn't improving.

After bringing him to our personal vet and having a couple of x-rays taken, Pyro was diagnosed with an overly steep Palmer angle. This caused his feet to be more upright, putting extra pressure on the coffin bone inside of the foot and making him sore. Barrak was back just in time to alter the angle, but changing the pitch back to normal doesn't fix a horse overnight. Pyro's foot was still inflamed and needed time to heal. Even though he was almost better by the time the vet came out to perform the pre-purchase exam, he was still sore enough to kill the sale. As much as the cash would have helped us out, we were even happier to still have Pyro as part of the herd. Despite him being sound again, he hadn't been able to train for a few weeks and wouldn't be ready for Tevis.

With Pyro still sore, my mom and I took our young horses on their first 50 at Creek to Peak, the second-to-last race before Tevis. Barrak and my dad took Quicksan and Goober to peak their training on the technical race. Since it was the first season of endurance racing for the horses my mom and I were riding, we didn't see the boys during the whole 50 miles. Coming into the finish an hour behind them, we arrived just before Barrak and my dad were due to show their horses for the Best Condition.

"How'd they do?" we asked.

"Quicksan did great and came in first!" Barrak said. "We left Pa and Goober at about 30 miles and came in ten minutes ahead of them. Goober had another bad day, and he barely got his completion because he was sore in his rear end again."

At the Best Condition showing an hour later, Goober was still sore. We had the vet draw blood for an assessment panel on Goober. After analyzing the immediate results, we determined that it was most likely not a muscle problem but might be more structural. The vet at the ride recommended that we have Goober examined by our veterinarian specializing in lameness when we got home.

Despite how well our four horses had been training early in the year, things just kept going downhill. The way things were heading, with Pyro and Goober lame, we would be lucky to make it to the starting line of Tevis with even one horse.

The fear of a career-ending injury for Goober loomed over us as we speculated on the causes of his lameness. A muscle cramp was the most common and easiest to fix, so we always jumped on that train, but there can be a million reasons why a horse is lame. What if Goober's OCD (osteochondritis dissecans) from when he was a yearling was flaring up? Perhaps it was something new, like a bone chip in his hock or stifle.

We scheduled a vet examination for Goober and hoped for the best, but feared the worst. Hopefully the results would offer a solution. If not, Goober wouldn't be able to go to Tevis.

As the vet looked him over, flexed his joints, and squeezed his feet, it was apparent that Goober was a little uncomfortable.

"So, what do you think?" my mom asked the vet after he had looked everything over.

"Well, his hocks are sore. It's fairly common in performance horses his age to get sore hocks."

"Okay. What do you suggest?"

"I would recommend injecting them with an anti-inflammatory steroid that will help with the inflammation and pain. It is similar to a cortisone injection for people."

"Will that fix it?" I asked, having a hard time believing that one simple injection could do the trick. "Does he have arthritis or a bone chip or something else going on?"

"It's doubtful that there's anything else going on," said the vet. "Goober's only ten, and I think the hocks are just inflamed and irritated right now. I would inject them and let the joints calm down for a few weeks. He should still be able to make it to Tevis."

Sticking a needle into the joint of a horse is one of the most stressful procedures for me. I'm always relieved that the vets know what they're doing, and it isn't me who has to insert the needle.

Goober fought the sedation and, despite getting groggy, was

determined to stay conscious. After giving him three times the usual amount of sedation, Goober finally relaxed enough that the vet felt comfortable penetrating the joint. Following a thorough scrubbing, lots of betadine suds, and sterilization, the vet inserted the needle precisely into Goober's hind joints, followed by an injection of the clear liquid. I held my breath during the whole process, knowing that if Goober moved his joint and the needle tip broke off, sore hocks would be the least of our worries.

Thankfully everything went well, and we were optimistic that the injections would solve Goober's lameness. I worried a bit about him entering Tevis so soon after this, but there was still time to make sure he could do it without hurting him. He sat out the last race before Tevis to allow the injection time to do its work. This last race was crucial to gauge how the horses were doing. Quicksan was thriving and seemed to still be on track for a successful Tevis run.

My dad took Goober out alone a few times after the procedure to check him out. He wanted to top off the horse's training and adjust his workouts to fit Goober's individual needs and get him ready for the start line. The time off had been good for Goober, and he was training stronger and more powerfully than he had all year.

A couple of weeks before Tevis, my dad brought up an idea he had mentioned a few times earlier.

"Sanoma, why don't you ride Goober at Tevis? I know you guys will do great. Between how Goober is training now and your lighter weight, you could have a really good chance at the win."

"I don't know," I said. "Who will you ride? I don't want to take your horse."

"I'll take Luke," he replied. "I'm curious to see how he will do. I've hardly ever ridden a horse as powerful as him."

"He's crazy and will probably fall off all those drop-offs," I said, laughing. "It's okay, just take Goober and I'll crew."

"How about you take Goober on a training ride and see how you get along," Pa suggested.

There were a bunch of reasons for me not to ride at Tevis that year. "I don't like the narrow trails," I admitted. "Besides, it's too late for the entry, and we would have to pay the extra-late sign-up fee. Also, Goober has a perfect record and came in with the 2nd place horse last year. And I don't have much experience competing at Tevis. I think it would just be best if you rode him."

"Don't feel any pressure to go for the win," my dad reassured me. "Just ride your race, and you'll do great. I want to see what Luke's got. It will be fun!"

I thought it over and was still a bit concerned about Pa riding Luke, but I agreed to at least do the next training ride with Goober.

Despite my dad's kind words, I still felt the pressure to do well. There were a lot of cons, but there were also a lot of pros. I was about 40 pounds lighter than my dad. Goober also had a different mentality when I rode him; he was more competitive and didn't hang back with me as much as he did with my father.

After riding Goober on one of the last training rides before Tevis, I remembered why I loved him so much and always had such a blast. He was easy to ride, laid back, and moved out really well. The injections had worked wonders and soothed all the inflammation that was causing the soreness. The vet had given us the green light, and I was excited and ready to take on the world with Goober as my partner. So, despite my fear of the Tevis trail and insecurity about my inexperience, I sent off my entry form with the late sign-up fee.

Luke was well-behaved, and in the weeks leading up to Tevis he didn't give us any reason to doubt that he would be manageable. Once we'd made up our minds to bring Luke, Quicksan, and Goober to Tevis, we were all stoked with the decision. We tapered the training, made the last few adjustments to tack, and took the horses on a couple of comfortable rides, mainly to get their energy out and fine-tune everything to get ready for the race we had been training for all year.

I never would have imagined that, eight years after picking up spindly, two-year-old Goober for free on Craigslist, he would be one of the strongest contenders at the world's most famous endurance race.

CHAPTER 11

No Turning Back

One week to go. A year's worth of preparation and training now came down to just a few long days of packing and preparing.

We analyzed the competition, studying the list of contenders, their horses' race records and strategies, and who we would have to keep a close eye on. The list was quite long.

We weren't the only ones who studied our competition. Everyone did, and I'm sure our names were pretty high up on their lists. Being the family that had consistently put horses in the top 10 for the last five years—and topping it off the previous year with a 100 percent completion rate and placing 2nd, 3rd, and 5th—I'm sure our competitors were keeping a sharp eye on us.

With my dad riding Luke, a horse that had never done a 100-mile race before, the pressure to represent our family's stables was on me and Barrak. Since Goober had completed Tevis twice more than Quicksan and had a perfect race record, I felt an immense responsibility to do well and live up to my family's name. We were the top endurance stables in the Northwest, and well-known across the country for our Tevis accomplishments.

The weeks after signing up for Tevis had flown by, and our training was mostly done. Mainly just the tedious preparations remained. We had to shave the horse's coats shorter and apply their footwear. We also had to pack for a week's worth of camping, not to mention all of our race gear. The point-to-point race required extra equipment since we wouldn't be able to return to the trailer for the vet holds.

My mom and I were in charge of packing everything while Barrak and my dad were busy gluing the rubber hoof boots onto the horses' feet. We usually ride with steel shoes on our horses, but for Tevis, we chose to ride them with the rubber glue-ons. They give extra traction and stay on quite well.

Applying the boots is a process. First, the foot is trimmed and then thoroughly cleaned before we use a flame torch to dry the foot and kill all the excess bacteria. The hoof needs to be virtually sterile for the glue to bond correctly. After the boot is prepared, the soft cushion glue is applied to the sole. The final, most critical step is bonding the boot to the hoof, using a glue product that sets up in less than 60 seconds. Once the boot is on, the horse shouldn't move for a couple of minutes to ensure a strong chemical bond between the hoof and the rubber boot.

While my mom and I were packing, the horses were getting their new shoes. They started with Luke, and everything was going well. The boots fit perfectly. However, being the first boot of the year, we forgot to pick up his opposite foot. While the glue was in the process of hardening, of course Luke moved his foot and broke the glue bond. His boot came off and left us with a sticky black mess. The unset glue ruined the boot, stuck to his foot, and made it impossible to sterilize it again so we could apply another boot.

We couldn't afford to have many spare boots on hand in case of mistakes, and we didn't have time to order another one since they're a special online order. Fortunately, Barrak was able to work his farrier magic and clean the boot and hoof enough to give it a second try. The glue took a bit longer to bond with the less-sterilized hoof and boot, but after some patience, Luke was ready to go. We made the best of the boot situation and finished off the three horses with their traction-safe glue-on boots.

We loaded boxes of race supplies onto the truck's flatbed, checking off items on our list as we went: food, water, and everything in-between. We were preparing to head south on Wednesday, giving us two days before the race on Saturday.

On Monday, we clipped the horses' coats shorter. After that, I trotted Goober out for my mom to watch. Based on his last couple of rides where he looked great, I was expecting him to look amazing with his new boots. As Goober trotted by my side, I could see he had a hitch in his gait. Again, it was his rear end. This was devastating.

He was still moving freely, so we assumed the issue was in the foot. I took him for a short ride through the neighborhood, and he seemed a little better afterward but still sore. I was crushed. Even if he could be sound for the vet-in, 100 miles is an impossibly long way to go if there is any pain in the foot.

Barrak pulled Goober's boot, trimmed the foot a little, and applied a smaller-sized boot that was left over from the previous year. We didn't have any other options beyond changing the boot, consulting our vet, and icing him. We hoped Goober would be better in a couple of days. It was too close to the race for any medication, as it would present itself in a drug test.

"Well, what should we do?" I asked my parents. "I could bring Mickey. He could probably finish if we go slow."

"He is probably in similar shape to Luke," my dad replied, "so we could ride together."

"But I'm not sure if I'm comfortable with Mickey when it comes to the Tevis trail drop-offs," I said, remembering the fatal accident from my first Tevis. "I'm sure he'd be fine, but I don't know if I would be. I was okay with Goober because he's more experienced, and when it counts, he pays attention to where his feet are."

"We could just go down with the two horses," Mom suggested. "That would be much less stressful traveling. If we brought Goober and he wasn't better by the vet-in, the crew could just take care of him during the race."

"We won't get a refund on my entry unless he vets-in lame," I said.

"I guess we can bring him along and hope he gets better by Friday afternoon," my dad said.

My mom finished his train of thought. "If he vets-in sound, you can ride him. If not, at least we get our entry fee back."

On Wednesday, we loaded up. We had done all we could for Goober. After driving about three and a half hours south, we unloaded the horses for a brief break to stretch their legs. I trotted Goober out again for my parents, and he still seemed a little sore but was doing much better. Deep down, I felt that if Goober didn't vet-in, it wouldn't be the end of the world. There was still part of me that didn't want to experience the steep drop-offs and pressure of racing Tevis.

We almost always had the same pre-Tevis routine: the route we took, where we stopped, and where we spent the night. Even though the drive to Tevis was just under nine hours in the car, it took us two days to get there when we hauled horses. We broke up the trip so the horses could rest better and be fully hydrated. The one time that we had changed our routine, our horses didn't perform as well, and that was when Pre and I had been pulled for dehydration.

On the first day of traveling, we stopped a few miles outside of Alturas, California. It was our tradition to stop at my family's favorite campground on the way to Tevis on Wednesday evening. A couple of miles down a gravel road off of Highway 395, there was a refreshing spring burbling up into the sage-brush that produced green range grass. We always unloaded the horses by the highway and rode up the gravel road to the camp spot. The two-mile ride settled the horses down after being in the trailer all day, and blew out a little of their bottled-up energy.

I held my breath as I mounted Goober, hoping he would be feeling better after some rest. After going a couple hundred feet up the road, Barrak and my parents said he looked 100 percent sound. Every once in a while, I thought I felt a hitch in his gait, but maybe it was just my paranoid imagination. I still had images in the back of my mind of Goober going lame halfway through the race. That would be more disappointing than not starting at all.

Arriving at our campsite, nestled under large cottonwood trees lining the stream's bank, I saw that my mom had already situated the trailer and was setting up camp. A lot of hunters used this campground during hunting season, but it was most-ly vacant during the hot summer. The creek flowing down the valley seemed out of place in the sea of desert around us. The horses settled into the log corral set up in the campground.

The waxing moon, chirping crickets, grazing horses, and race strategizing at dinner made for an indescribable atmosphere. We discussed the odds of the race and how well we expected each horse to do. The anticipation, excitement, and anxiety we were feeling would leave a great impression on this camp spot's memories.

Everything we had done, the things we had worked so hard for, all boiled down to one day. Very soon, it would all be behind us. No matter what happened on race day, we would have some stories to tell.

On Thursday morning, we tacked up, broke camp, and rode

the horses back to the highway while my mom drove the loaded truck and trailer. It would be a new day of traveling, much shorter than the previous day. We would go through Reno, Nevada, and on the busy I-80 freeway into California. After a hectic border check where we had to show our horses' vet-issued health certificates to the strict border patrol, we were on our way. We were only hours away from our destination and the start of the race.

As the freeway led us past Donner Pass and deeper into the Sierras, I thought about this landscape, which had lured gold-hungry miners. In those days, the prospects of independence and free land drove the wagon trains west; today, it was racing horses across these same mountains that brought competitors from as far away as the East Coast and even other countries.

Emerging into cell service again, my mom received a new voicemail from Tal, a fellow racer who was 17 years old and hoped to ride in the top 10. Since he was under 18, he was searching for a sponsor to ride with. He asked if my dad would sponsor him. We talked about it on the drive as we made our way farther south. We decided to take him for a ride and, if his horse matched well with ours, my dad would sponsor him. Remembering being in this situation years ago, when the Fords were willing to sponsor 13-year-old Barrak, we were happy to be able to pay it forward.

Driving through Truckee, a bustling mountain town, the smell of pine trees mixed with burgers on the grill for lunch filled the truck's cab. Tourists were walking the historic sidewalks and browsing quaint shops with sale racks sitting out front. The lively town oozed with freshness, but we weren't there to see Truckee. We were simply driving through. After passing through a couple of neighborhoods, we made our way to the start of the Western States 100.

We parked the truck six miles before the camp to unload the horses. From there, we would saddle up and follow behind the truck the rest of the way. The sun was shining, the pine trees freshened the air, and we were enjoying the slightly cooler temperature at the higher elevation as we rode behind the trailer. It was impossible to be anything but happy. Our horses felt great and Goober wasn't giving any signs of being sore, but we still took it slow to make sure he didn't strain anything. By the time we made it to the top, the horses were sweaty and ready to settle in for the evening.

We set up our camp and hung the hammocks and, with dinner sizzling on the propane grill, our good friends Brian, Andrea, their daughter, Michaela, and her friend, Sarah, arrived as crew. We handed Michaela and Sarah a couple of "Blakeley Endurance Stable" shirts and asked Brian and Andrea if they still had their team T-shirts from last year.

"Yep, they're somewhere in there," Brian said, pointing toward the SUV that was filled with crewing gear and camping equipment.

"If things go south, just turn the shirts inside out to the 'Joe's Auto Body' logo," Pa joked.

On Friday morning, we headed to the Tevis packet pickup and received our vet cards and tickets to enter pen one and start in the first wave of 60 horses. Along with many different vendors and sponsors was a booth advertising helicopter insurance. Nothing takes the wind out of your sails like being asked if you need helicopter insurance.

Between ongoing preparations and riding with Tal, the time to present our horses for the vet arrived before we knew it. I hopped on Goober bareback and trotted him around for a while to make sure he was warmed up for the vet. Then I nervously waited for our turn in line, knowing the results of the vet's exam would impact our ride tomorrow.

"Everything looks good," the vet told me.

I wasn't sure whether to be happy or disappointed, knowing nothing was left to stop me from racing the next day. Our race had a good chance of being cut short at any time, but I was still excited to have at least made it to the start line.

"Head over to the volunteers." The vet pointed toward a group of people with bright-blue T-shirts that read 'Tevis Cup Volunteer.' "They will write your rider number on your horse and then, if you will, head to the scales to weigh your horse for a research project."

"Okay, thanks!" I smiled at the vet.

"Good luck tomorrow," he said, signaling for the next horse in line to step up for its vet exam.

After the pre-ride briefing, the race director ended his talk with, "We'll see you all tomorrow at the start line. Have a good night." As he said that, it hit me like a ton of bricks that, in less than 12 hours, we would be racing away. That little nervous voice in my head still wondered if Goober and I would make it. My heart rate rose, and I could feel the excitement and anxiety as we made our way back to camp for a final night of rest.

CHAPTER 12

Let the Race Begin

Throughout the night, I tossed and turned in my sleeping bag, checking the time on my phone every couple of hours.

At 2:00 AM, about an hour before I had to get up, I closed my eyes and tried to ease my nerves and find some valuable rest. I dozed a couple of times. Finally, at around 3:15, I woke up for good. There was no way I was going to get any more sleep, so I turned off my alarm and stepped out of the tent into the dark forest. Looking up past the tall pines at thousands of twinkling stars, I felt mesmerized for a few brief moments before contemplating how to be most effective until the start of the race at 5:15 AM.

I wandered toward our three horses that were happily munching on hay. They were calm and ready to tackle the challenging day that lay ahead of them. My body quivered as I realized what stood before me. From my other three Tevis experiences, I was aware of just how demanding this race was. I was also feeling the pressure of riding a horse who had a perfect record.

Our camp came alive as the tea kettle started hissing. We folded up our tents and took down the hammocks. At 4:20, we started prepping the horses with our pre-prepared tack. The final part of breaking camp involved taking down the horse's corral, winding up the climbing rope that contained them.

Kneeling next to Goober, I fastened his leg boots. They protected his lower limbs from things he might hit on the trail, such as bushes, rocks, or fallen trees. They would also protect him if he bumped his other leg while trying to avoid an obstacle. I ran my hand gently down Goober's muscled leg. I could feel the powerful racehorse's energy. He was here for business, and he was ready.

After securing his final boot, I gently asked him to open his mouth for the bit. I knew Goober would be a handful at the start, and I wanted to make sure I was in control. I opted to have him in a bit for the first 36 miles, after which I figured he'd be calm enough for the hackamore.

We led our horses out to the road and shone our lamps over them for a final gear check. We confirmed we had our pen one tickets and vet cards, and mounted up. Once astride, we had to get the horses moving to prevent a tie-up. We headed away from the start, down the well-maintained gravel road into the darkness.

Tal joined us as we warmed up the horses. His horse had matched well with ours, so my dad had agreed to sponsor him. The gray gravel reflected the full moon, which cast shadows of our four horses. We talked race strategy as we headed back to the start, pulling our bandanas up over our noses to protect against the dust.

"Rider numbers?" the timer called out to us.

"Our numbers are 3, 5, and 203," I called out for my dad, Barrak, and myself. I halted Goober to hand her the tickets needed to get into pen one. My red headlamp light illuminated the dust, anxious horse whinnies, and tense riders, bringing butterflies swirling to my stomach. I pulled my bandana up higher on my nose, breathed deeply into the cotton, and followed Barrak and Quicksan into the crowd.

We kept the horses milling around the forest, riding down a narrow circular trail through the woods to an area where everyone else was warming up their horses.

"We just have to keep moving," my dad called back to us. Luke was getting more and more worked up.

We always tried to be in the group of the first horses on the road at the official start of the race, about a mile from the trailhead. The lap in the woods brought us back to the milling area. I looked at my watch. 4:56.

"We have four minutes till the road opens to head towards the start," I said.

"I think we have time for another lap," my dad said as Luke started prancing.

We followed Luke and my dad back into the woods. About halfway through the lap, dread came over us as we realized we wouldn't make it back in time for the controlled start at the official beginning of the race.

Our tension built and made for a grim mood as we popped out of the woods and caught the tail end of the 60 horses heading up the road to the official start line. We had lost crucial time and positions, as places to pass other horses were sparse in the first few miles.

The moon permitted enough light to see the rows of horses ahead of us as we worked our way past the tail-end horses. We slipped by several of them, worming our way to the front whenever possible. The half-mile controlled start to where the race actually began went by quickly, and we tried to make up a few places. Finally, the horses in front stopped, and eventually we came to a standstill.

The experienced Goober stood patiently as a restless vibe spread through the other horses. The silence and anticipation made my stomach ache. The minutes seemed like hours as the eager horses moved around, switching positions and pawing.

"Stick close to Barrak, and if we get separated, just keep

going," my dad instructed, just before the ride manager announced, "Trail's open. See y'all in Auburn."

The spark reached the gunpowder, and Quicksan shot toward the trail like a cannonball. Goober was right behind her, glued to her tail as they both cut in front of several horses. Even though I tried to keep Goober in a trot, he quickly fell into a gallop to keep up with traffic. Half out of control and blinded by the thick dust, I held on, waiting for an incline so the horses would space out a little and settle down. I lost sight of my dad and Tal seconds into the race. I hoped they were okay, but I needed to concentrate entirely on Goober and myself.

It was still dark as we rode down the familiar trail. Goober fell into a robust and fast trot, and a couple of miles in, everything settled down a little. The horses were pulling hard but not wasting any extra energy. Dawn began to lighten the trail as we emerged into some thickly wooded switchbacks. Following the narrow path that wound up the hillside, we made our way to Squaw Valley. Under normal circumstances, the first climb would seem like a hefty incline, but nobody even batted an eye at this one, considering the much steeper climbs ahead.

Goober began sweating lightly, and despite the early morning, it already seemed hot and muggy. The air clung to my skin as we made our way deeper into the Sierra Mountains. The sun started coming up, and we were able to identify the competition in front of us. Barrak and I whispered back and forth in German, our secret language, as we named off serious competitors that were surprisingly only a few horses in front of us.

Past the first webcast station and across the Truckee River, we were again climbing switchbacks through the forest as we continued towards Auburn. Rounding the bend revealed a breathtaking view of Squaw Valley below us. The sun shone on the side of the valley opposite us but hadn't quite topped the hill, leaving us riding in the shade.

"Oh my gosh, oh my gosh, oh my gosh," I murmured, trying to stay calm as the trail narrowed next to the hillside below. There was nothing to stop my horse or me from sliding down. Before this point, there had been trees that would have blocked a fall; now, it was just a barren hillside lying below us. I knew Goober would keep his feet on the trail, but I could feel the panic well up inside of me as I realized the worst of the drop-offs and steep mountain trails were yet to come.

We continued along the hillside parallel to Squaw Valley, under the ski lifts, and past the section of trail where my dad's stirrup had broken four years earlier. I thought of all the what-ifs with this trail. Despite how hard I tried to concentrate on Goober and my race, the worry wasn't something I could just push away. Just like in chess, you always have to think several moves ahead to stay on top. It was the over-analyzing, worry, and strategizing that had gotten me to where I was, at the front of the race.

The trail merged with the road that led the horse-and-rider teams to the Olympic Ski Village and the second webcast station. Goober was pulling hard, and I was glad I had chosen to use his bit. I continually reminded him that we had another 90 miles to go and a long day ahead of us.

"Slow down!" Barrak told me. "This is a long climb."

"I'm trying, but Goober is feeling good."

I gave the reins resistance as we trotted past the horses ahead of us. We passed Jeremy and Heather Reynolds, who were walking up the road. I made eye contact with Barrak. We both had the same thought—that we were pushing too soon. But there were still about six racers in front of us, and our horses felt good.

We knew they could handle it. The Reynoldses had their own strategy.

Riding past the race's highest point, Watson Monument, I took one last glance behind me. The golden sun had come up and was casting its rays on the valleys below. Lake Tahoe looked extra blue, and for a brief second, I was able to detach myself from the task at hand and admire the view before snapping back to reality.

Protected by the elevation and shade, we ascended into the Granite Chief wilderness. A few snowdrifts had yet to melt, and everything seemed a couple of months behind as we rode by lush grasses, the kind that had already browned in the lower country. The snowmelt also formed bogs that we had to navigate, and watered the yellow sunflowers and other mountain foliage. There were only a couple of horses in front of us, and Barrak was on foot, running next to Quicksan. Where the trail was too rocky or wet for us to trot, we slowed to a walk, and the horses munched on fresh fuel. A hungry horse is always a good sign in a race.

An hour further down the trail, we came upon our first vet check. It was about 20 miles in, and it was just a trot-by. The vets were there to watch the horses ride by, and if they saw anything concerning, they would call you back for a closer look.

I thought I felt something. *Yep, Goober is definitely sore. The vet is going to ask me to stop.* My paranoia was getting the better of me.

"Looks good," the vet called.

I exhaled in relief. One stop down. Goober was moving well, and I just tried to focus on getting through one vet check at a time.

We continued down the trail, riding atop a ridge. The granite transitioned to volcanic rock as the trail ascended once again, only about 30 feet up the volcanic mass known as Cougar Rock.

This year, I was determined to ride up it. After the horse fell off Cougar Rock and died right in front of me during my first Tevis, I had somehow mustered up the courage to climb up it in 2015, and this year all I had to do was follow Quicksan up. I had nothing to worry about; Goober had done it three times, and was officially an old pro at climbing Cougar Rock.

After giving Quicksan space to be alone for the iconic picture, I started to head up after her. Suddenly, she turned around and faced us. I panicked and jumped off Goober. He got a little upset that we had to stop, and tugged to continue. I tried to get back on him again to keep going, but he wouldn't stand still. I told myself to calm down. Even though Goober probably wouldn't do anything stupid, I took him by his halter and ran with him on foot around Cougar Rock on the bypass trail, where I met Barrak and Quicksan on the other side.

I was disappointed in myself for not facing my fears. Goober would have been just fine, and we would have gotten a cool picture because he was such a handsome boy. During the next few miles, I mulled over how I should have just waited the extra five seconds to get back on Goober instead of walking on. *Maybe it was for the best. Cougar Rock is steep, Goober could have irritated his leg and possibly made himself sore.* Exhaling, I pushed the past out of my mind along with the fresh mountain air.

We moved along at a nice clip now, only half a mile from Red Star Ridge, where the vets would perform their first thorough examination. We were riding with Lindsay Fisher and Monk, a very well-known horse that had raced for the U.S. endurance team overseas and held the fastest 100-mile record in the United States. Monk had also finished Tevis in the top 10 four years in a row.

The veteran racehorse was pranced sideways and looked unhappy as some riders who usually don't ride up front blew past us. As they charged up the road, I was glad we were riding with Lindsay, who knew the trail well. The course veered to the left, and had she not pointed out the turn, we would have continued up the wrong road, blindly following the other riders who weren't looking at the trail markers.

"The trail turns here!" we shouted after them, but they were out of sight by the time we reached the fork in the road.

"Oh well," Lindsay said, shrugging. "I guess they'll realize they are off-trail fairly soon, when there aren't any more marker ribbons on that road."

As we vetted through Red Star, I saw my dad and Tal come into the check behind the group that had missed the turn. I was relieved to see that they were okay. Luke looked excellent and not too worked up.

Barrak came through the vet exam a few minutes behind us, and Goober used that extra time to munch some hay. Another check down!

"Well, shall we head out?" I asked Barrak.

"Maybe just let Quicksan eat for a couple more minutes," he suggested.

As our journey to the next stop continued, we rode along a dirt road that connected Robinson Flats with Red Star Ridge. The horses were usually a little faster on this stretch than we would have liked, but it was one of the few spots where we could make up time and move out faster. The four or five horses in our small group galloped down the road, urging each other along and feeling good. I eased Goober into an extended trot, which kept his weight more evenly balanced on all four legs. Galloping is more comfortable but can cause a horse to push more on a specific leg. Glancing at my Garmin watch, I smiled when I saw that Goober was pushing a 15 mile-per-hour trot next to horses who were stretching out and galloping.

The eight miles between the two vet stops went by quickly, and within 43 minutes, our little group had arrived at Robinson. Until your hour hold starts, it is vital to cool your horse and not waste any time getting to the pulser. My crew came running to help. I had already stripped off my tack and was leading Goober to the water tank. Goober guzzled the water as I lightly sponged him so as not to disrupt his hydrating. He finished drinking, and our crew dumped water on him more heavily.

Quicksan needed another minute to hydrate before heading to the pulse box.

"Is Quicksan ready to go pulse?" I asked.

"Yeah, I'll be right behind you," Barrak replied.

Based on how unfazed he looked, I knew Goober had probably already reached pulse criteria, so I took him into the pulse box. We emerged and headed to the vet area just as quickly as we entered, except the hour countdown had already begun.

"How's your ride going?" the vet asked.

"It's amazing! This country is so beautiful, and my horse is feeling great. We're having a blast."

The vet smiled as he walked around Goober, checking all his vitals. "Can you give me a trot to the end of the chalk lane?"

"Mm-hmm." I tried to keep Goober and myself within the chalk boundary as I trotted him out in hand for the vet to watch. *What if he catches something wrong with Goober?*

But my fears were over in a few seconds.

"He looks good," the vet said as his scribe handed my vet card back. "We'll see you down the trail."

My mom led us to the spot on top of a small hill shaded by a large pine tree. There, our crew had set up a rest stop with everything the horses and riders needed. After making sure the two horses were comfortable, I stretched and sat on a fallen ponderosa for a bit, munching on some M&Ms and dried fruit. The brilliant sun shone down on us and dried the sweaty horses. At 10:30 AM, it was already warm.

In my mind, I liked to break Tevis into thirds. The first third was the wilderness: Cougar Rock, Elephant's Trunk, and Red Star Ridge. The second was the canyons, which meant heat, sweat, and dust. The final third consisted of lots of declines, riding in the dark, and crossing the American River.

I re-packed my saddlebags for the second third of the race, refilling my bottle of Goober's electrolytes and adding water bottles and electrolytes for myself, sponges, and lighter gear. I replaced my bit with the hackamore and swapped out Goober's wet saddle pad for a dry one.

"Quicksan isn't doing too great," Barrak mentioned as his horse picked at the alfalfa with less of an appetite than Goober.

"She looks fine to me," I said. "How were her vet scores?" I hoped she was okay because I did not want to go on by myself, especially this early in the race.

"The vet said she looked fine, but she doesn't seem like her usual beasty self." Barrak sounded concerned. He knew his horse well.

"We'll keep an eye on her and see how she does during the hour," Mom said, giving Quicksan some extra attention.

A little later, my dad came in and caught us up on his version of the beginning of the race. Unfortunately, Tal's horse couldn't keep up with Luke and had pulsed down a few minutes behind. My dad had found another sponsor who was willing to take Tal, and they'd gone their separate ways.

We all exchanged worried glances as Quicksan urinated and the color appeared a bit darker than usual. That was a bad sign, especially this early in the race.

"Do you think she had a muscle tie-up from getting too anxious at the start?" my mom asked as we examined her closer.

"No, she pulsed right down, and everything else seems fine," Barrak said. "She drank when we came in, so I don't think she's dehydrated. We'll take it easy and see what happens."

With only seven minutes left of our hour hold, the chaos started again as our crew ran around, securing everything and rechecking to make sure we were set for the next 32 miles—the most demanding section of trail.

There were only two horses and riders ahead of me and Barrak: Karen Donnelly and Gwen Hall. Karen and her horse had won Tevis before, and Gwen was a top racer who had also ridden for the U.S. team at the World Championships. As we continued down the dirt road that led us toward the Dusty Corners water stop, we caught sight of Gwen and Karen ahead as the road made a sweeping turn, revealing itself below.

Barrak and I rode at our own pace and tried not to be influenced by Karen, Gwen or the others passing by us. As it worked out, by the time we reached Dusty Corners we had caught up with them, and soon found ourselves riding with the two women on their gray horses.

The course led us off the broad road and redirected us to a powdery, strenuous road. The five miles from Dusty Corners to the Last Chance vet check was one of my least favorite sections of the race. The footing was tough, deep dirt with roots hidden just under the dust layer, with scrawny pine trees surrounding the trail. The sun beat down on us there, and the course was disengaging. With no scenic views and the horses shuffling along the fairly level road, my mind began to drift elsewhere on this section of trail. Nevertheless, I re-secured my bandana and plunged ahead.

This year, the trail had been diverted from the typical route because range cows had damaged the original single-track trail. I was relieved to stay on the road to Last Chance and avoid

Pucker Point, the biggest drop-off on the course. Pucker Point was a sheer cliff, dropping 1,000 feet down to the American River below. It was unsettling to ride by those steep drop-offs, and I was glad to bypass the narrow trail. Plus, we could move out nicely and make extra time on the wider road.

After we'd arrived at Last Chance and the third vet check, a big group of horses and riders came in right behind us. My dad was with them.

"Wow, you guys made good time," I said.

"How's Luke doing?" Barrak asked.

"He's doing great!" Pa replied. "Lindsay and I were riding together. Luke was a little out of control at one point on that road coming out of Robinson, and we were running at 19 miles an hour."

Knowing Luke, I wasn't surprised that he'd taken advantage of not having a bit and running away with my dad.

The line for the vet at Last Chance was moving slowly. I always like to get the vet exam out of the way and have some peace of mind, so I was a little impatient as we waited for the line to dwindle. Finally, we passed the vet check with ease and I rode off with Barrak and my dad. So far, things were going well.

"Off into the abyss!" I joked as we started our descent down the first of the three canyons. My dad and Barrak were on foot, running as they led their horses down.

"You can stay on Goober," my dad told me. "It'll be faster, and you won't be doing him much good since he is used to my extra weight."

So I rode Goober and we led the way down, switchback after switchback. Someone was right below us. I could hear them, but the overgrown scrub oak blocked the view from the switchbacks above and below. About two-thirds of the way down the canyon, we heard the roar of the river echoing below us, making it sound as though we should be at the bottom in no time. The bottom-less pit into the first canyon just kept sinking as the river got louder with each switchback.

When we finally reached the bottom of the canyon, two op-tions lay ahead of us as the trail split: we could ford the river or ride across the swinging bridge. We chose the bridge. Cross-ing the bridge saves time, and a few yards down the course is a stream that pools next to the trail. Goober drank and tanked up for our ascent.

"You are going to be faster than us since we are taking it up on foot, so just go ahead and don't wait for us," my dad instruct-ed me.

"Are you sure? I can walk a little, too."

"Just stay on, and we'll see you at the Devil's Thumb," my dad told me firmly, knowing I didn't want to go on alone.

Power-walking up the steep switchbacks, Goober and I ar-rived at Devil's Thumb a few minutes ahead of the boys and right behind Lindsay and Monk. The cold water in the shade of the towering pines offered much relief to the hot horses. Goober seemed unfazed by the first canyon, despite the strenuous climb, and was way more concerned that Quicksan was not with him. His high-pitched whinnies echoed through the stillness of the water stop.

"Do you need us to hold your horse?" some helpful volun-teers offered.

"I'm okay, thanks!" I replied.

"Do you want us to refill your water bottles," another volun-teer asked, "or do you want some watermelon?"

I handed the volunteers my water bottles, and they returned with ice-cold water and a few slices of watermelon. Normally, I would eat the red part of the watermelon and give Goober the rind, but we both got our own whole slice on race day, and he appreciated the sweet fruit as the juice dripped off his whiskers.

"I'll see you guys at Deadwood," I called over my shoulder to Barrak and my dad. I was riding out of the refreshing water stop just as they arrived.

The mile and a half of gradual terrain to Deadwood was a relief. We didn't even notice the small inclines or declines after hauling out of that last canyon.

"His pulse is 48 beats per minute, and he seems to be doing well," the vet remarked at the Deadwood vet check.

"He is feeling great," I told the vet, "though he's not too happy to be without his running mate, Quicksan."

I let Goober rest and munch on some hay while I waited for Barrak and my dad.

"Would you mind holding my horse and just make sure he keeps eating?" I asked one of the volunteers as Barrak and my dad came into the check.

"You lost a boot," I told my dad as I noticed Luke's naked front right foot.

"Oh, great." My dad sighed.

"I think I saw it not too far back," Barrak said. "I just figured it was somebody else's." He reassured my dad that Luke's foot shouldn't be too sore, since he hadn't been barefoot for very long.

"It's the first boot we put on, the one that we messed up," Pa said. "Let's just hope we don't lose another. I only have one spare."

"I'll ask around for a screwdriver to put the spare on," I offered as my dad tried to slip on the tight boot before heading to the vet.

I was getting ready to head out again, this time alone. I would most likely be by myself for the rest of the ride. Quicksan was having an off day, so Pa and Barrak were going to slow down. I glanced back and saw that they were feeding their horses near the tree where, four years earlier, my race had been cut short. I smiled to myself as I remembered my past experiences at this hold. My horse had been pulled because he'd become dehydrated. *I've come a long way as a rider in these four years since,* I thought. Goober was way stronger, and I didn't have to worry about our race ending with him on IV fluids.

Mounting up, Goober and I were both sad to leave our friends, especially with another 45 miles to go by ourselves. Goober was determined to stay with Quicksan and at first refused to go on. I knew he wasn't tired yet, just stubborn.

Heading into the second canyon, Goober was riding with his brakes on. *It's going to be a long 45 miles if I have to encourage him the whole way to Auburn.*

We were slowly trotting down a steep slope when another horse caught up to us. I had no idea who the young rider was and hadn't recalled seeing her before. Then again, I was busy at the last hold and hadn't noticed who else was at the vet check.

The rider, Haley, was a fun partner on the trail, and we chatted our way down the second canyon. It turned out that we had a similar ride plan for the canyons. I knew her from her reputation and social media, but this was my first time meeting her in person. She was a breath of fresh air, and her lively and upbeat disposition helped pull my head together and forget about the stress of riding alone. I was relieved to share the responsibility of leading with another horse.

"I just got my nails done to match my tack and the stable colors of my horse," Haley said in her sweet Texas accent.

"Aww, they look so cute," I said from behind her. I bit my lip, looking at my own nails that were covered in dirt, trail dust, sweat, and sticky black electrolytes.

It wasn't until Haley mentioned the stable colors that I made the connection of whose horse she was riding. I knew Ogee's owners only by reputation, but I suddenly took her more seriously as a competitor. Ogee would be a tough horse to compete against, especially with a rider that weighed next to nothing.

This was Haley's first 100-mile race, and I respected her, but felt terrible for her because she had the wrong gear for the steep terrain. Her saddle had some exaggerated knee rolls on it that made my knees sore just thinking of the chafing she was experiencing.

Despite expressing her hopes of finding a replacement saddle, she had a positive attitude and I enjoyed having someone to ride with as we entered the most demanding section of trail. At the bottom of El Dorado Canyon, we crossed the bridge, and I dismounted. My feet were happy to have some solid footing, taking a break from bracing against the stirrups. The volunteers were pumping cool water out of the El Dorado River into an easy-access tank. I sponged Goober and cooled him. Haley had lost her sponge, so I cooled her horse as well.

Bracing for the second ascent, this one longer than the previous, we hit it at a power walk. Goober and Haley's horse, Ogee, took turns leading. The endless canyon dragged on as the manzanitas grew more plentiful and eucalyptus replaced the scrub oak.

Coming into Michigan Bluff, Goober was starting to embarrass me with his high-pitched whinnying, looking for Quicksan. Luckily the crew was there and helped me cool him off.

"How's Goober look?" I asked my mom.

"He looks really good! Where is Barrak?"

"He pulled back with Pa. Quicksan isn't doing too great." I could see the worry on Mom's face. "But Barrak is taking good care of her, and she seemed okay. She just needs to go a little slower."

We left the water stop at Michigan Bluff with Haley and Ogee and continued through the small town. About half a mile before Piper Junction, I decided to ease back and let her go on ahead. I knew we still had another canyon ahead, and I didn't want to push Goober too hard into the vet check. I was surprised to see that all the competitors ahead of us were still at the hold when we arrived. Maybe I was biased, but Goober seemed fresher than the other five horses at that check.

"Do you want a courtesy pulse?" one of the volunteers asked once Goober had rehydrated.

"Sure, that would be great," I answered as I sponged Goober down.

The volunteer measured his heart rate. "It's 68. Pulse criteria is 64. Do you want me to check again?"

"No thanks! I'm sure he will be 64 by the time we walk over to the vets."

And he was.

I was shocked to learn that Goober was the first horse vetted through. We could leave anytime, and we only had four miles to our second one-hour mandatory hold.

The volunteers were all so helpful and fed Goober while I was cooling him. They also brought me water and reminded me to drink and take care of myself, which I had neglected to do throughout the day.

About a half-mile out of Piper, I remembered to electrolyte Goober. Usually I would have done this at the water tank as I left a vet check, but I was chatting with the out-timers and completely forgot. So, I let Goober walk and poured the sticky electrolytes into my syringe. The molasses and honey made them more palatable, but also messier.

"Whoa, boy." I brought Goober to a stop and pulled his head over to my right leg. I held up his lip with my left hand

and squirted the diluted salts into his mouth with my right. Even though they don't taste horrible, horses try to avoid them, so I was extra-proud of Goober for not fighting me and saving us time. I put him back into a trot and headed down our last canyon. I carefully crossed the creek at Volcano Canyon, very aware that this was where my race had ended with Sporty three years ago.

As soon as we hit Bath Road, Goober knew where we were, and he picked it up to a nice vigorous trot right into Forest Hill. We rode past the spectators, who cheered and applauded as Goober powered up the paved road.

We came into the vet stop in 4th place behind Karen Donnelly, Lindsay Fisher, and Haley. The water was too warm to cool Goober's body temperature, so I made my way straight to the pulsers to start my hold time. Even though we came into Forest Hill in 4th place, his heart rate reached pulse criteria ahead of the other two riders, so we could leave in 2nd place behind Karen.

"You've done a good job taking care of him today," the vet said. He was impressed with how fresh Goober looked.

"Thanks!" I replied as I exhaled a sigh of relief. "He's doing well." The hard part was finally over, and not once had a vet mentioned that Goober was sore.

Walking past the chaos to my crew's camp, I looked to my mom again for some reassurance. "How does he look?" I asked.

"He looks awesome," Mom assured me.

"Are you sure?" I asked. I don't know what I was expecting her to say—"Just kidding, you should pull." It was obvious that Goober was doing well.

While picking at some food and forcing myself to drink some water, I asked my mom, "What do you think should be my game plan?"

"Well, the Reynolds are coming," my mom warned. "They passed Barrak and Pa and are moving up fast."

Goober ate well but was irritated with me. He knocked over his bucket of oats and then looked at me to make sure I knew he was upset that he was all alone. Then he just about blew out my eardrums calling for his friend.

"You know, Goober is just taking advantage of you," Mom said. "He's unruly, bored, and throwing a tantrum. He had excellent vet scores, and the vet said you have taken good care of him. You need to be firm and let him know you aren't messing around. He needs to work a little." My mom's frank assurance did me some good.

There's no need to worry. Just push Goober a little and get his respect. I took my mom's advice to heart and was ready to head out again.

As I started toward the out-timer, Barrak and my dad were just arriving. I had made an hour on them over nine miles. As much as I wanted to talk with them and ask how their race was going, I didn't have time. It was too late, though; Goober had already seen Quicksan and didn't want to leave without her.

I got on Goober to head out again, but he planted his feet and refused to go on alone. I hopped off and ran him out on foot, frustrated but not wanting to deal with his attitude. A few hundred yards out of the vet check, and after a sufficient warm-up from the rest, I hopped back on and asked Goober for a comfortable gallop down the road, through the town of Forest Hill.

A few miles down the trail, our riding partner, Haley, caught up to us again. I enjoyed riding with her and was happy for the cheerful company. Goober, however, was losing interest and disliked the downhills, which was pretty much the last 36 miles of Tevis.

At the 75-mile point, we were gaining on Karen, and at times we could see her dust ahead of us. It was my first time experiencing this section of the trail in daylight. The grinding switchbacks dragged on, and Goober and I were both ready for some level ground.

As we neared the American River and rode parallel to it, the trail became hilly and consisted of more inclines. I let Goober walk the uphills, but he strolled along at a frustratingly mellow pace. We were still in a race, and he was starting to try my exhausted nerves with his laid-back attitude.

"Can you just walk in a straight line?" I begged him as I hopped off and dragged him up the hill behind me. Haley's horse wasn't helping his motivation, and was laid-back herself. I was surprised that our other competitors hadn't caught us yet.

I stayed ahead of Goober as we gained speed going down the decline. I realized how little care I'd been giving to myself all day, and I now had a massive side ache and felt lightheaded. I blocked the pain and focused on letting gravity work on propelling me and Goober forward. The hill was longer than I anticipated, but I had gained a little ground by the time we reached the bottom. Remounting and getting a little more serious with Goober, we continued down the trail parallel to the American River with Haley close behind.

The moisture here produced cooler, fresher air, and Goober got a second wind. We were finally moving nicely out again, and I realized just how much we had dilly-dallied. There was a nice patch of grass where my mom had suggested I let Goober graze. But after a few mouthfuls of grass, we would be wasting time by staying any longer.

"Is he running with his hind end a little to the left?" I asked Haley, who was following us.

"No, he looks straight to me," she said.

I wasn't sure if I was imagining things or just so used to straightening Goober all day. My calves were aching from all the leg pressure. Actually, every muscle in my body ached. I quickly rid my thoughts of the pain and focused on what I was there to do. We had three more vet checks to get our completion.

We must be getting close to Francisco's. I checked my watch, and we were right on schedule to be arriving at any minute. The road widened, and as we crossed a cement bridge with a few dumpsters at the side, Goober gave a big spook. I urged him forward and refocused him. Rounding the corner, we spotted the third-to-last vet check.

Francisco's was the vet check where the rubber hit the road. As the sun was setting behind the foothills of the Sierra Mountains, making its way for the Pacific, my next move at this vet check would play a vital role in the outcome of the race.

CHAPTER 13

Sunset at Francisco's and Bringing It Home

I hopped off Goober and jogged alongside him into the vet check. As the day grew longer, my mental endurance was kicking in, but I still had to force myself to keep moving forward. To be efficient, I made a mental checklist while taking in the scene at the check. *Water trough, a bite of hay for Goober, and then to the vet.*

Karen and her gray horse were getting ready to head out again. I should have noted what time she left, but I was distracted by a cluster of seven horses coming into the vet check. Watching the seven riders enter, my heart sank. They were all big names, each a serious contender for the win. Everybody had an impressive ride record; most of the group had at least been in the top 10 at Tevis before, and some had won. I knew that Goober had placed 3rd the year before with my dad and would be able to keep up with the group, but my own insecurities of never placing above 42nd at Tevis weighed heavily on me.

Francisco's was one of the most crucial vet stops, and timing was everything. The horse-and-rider teams that entered the vet stop had a special and somewhat solemn aura about them. It was brutal from here on out, and everyone knew it. We learned that 59 horses and riders had already been pulled at the vet stops prior to Francisco's.

Goober and I vetted through right away. He was perky and still looking good. I just needed to get some food into him and give him a little break.

"Can I help hold your horse or get you anything?" a friendly volunteer asked.

"Yeah, that would be great. Do you have any food that I could eat?" I thought back to how lightheaded I'd felt dragging Goober down the hill.

"We have some peanut butter sandwiches," the volunteer offered.

"Anything else?" I asked. The thought of peanut butter dried my mouth.

"I'm sorry, I can hold your horse and you can look at the food table, but I don't think it's all set up yet."

"Thanks. I have to eat something, so I guess that's better than nothing."

The peanut butter sandwich glued my dry mouth together, and the white bread wouldn't go down my throat. I drank, but the water hurt my empty stomach. I hated wasting food, but I couldn't down the much-needed nutrients. I dropped the remaining sandwich into the tall, dry grass, knowing some squirrel or bird would appreciate it. *Only 15 more miles. I can eat and drink at the finish.*

I made a game plan. Goober was eating, but he had enough fuel in him that, at this point, he was just storing reserves. I briefly scanned the competition. There were several untacked horses and a couple of riders waiting in line for the vet. The Reynolds were running around, sorting out a boot malfunction. Nobody even noticed as I grabbed a flake of hay and led Goober toward the out-timers.

The sun was now setting. I stopped for a brief moment to consider where we were and how far we'd come. Eighty-five miles down, and here I was, the second rider getting ready to leave Francisco's vet check. I didn't want to underestimate the last 15 miles as I took in the scene before us: commotion, everyone in their own race.

This was the calm before the storm. I knew it wouldn't be long before I was noticed, and a herd of competitive horses and their riders would try to catch us and most likely overtake us.

I walked to the out-timers and handed them my time card. "I'm number 203, and I'm heading out," I told them.

I continued down the trail on foot, leading Goober and letting him eat the alfalfa I held in my arm. Then, after crossing a creek at the bottom of the hill, I remounted him just as one of the eight horses behind us caught up. We continued on and up the gravel road together. Goober was leading as the racecourse turned into a narrow single-track trail. He was about halfway down the trail when Jeremy Reynolds came galloping up behind us.

"Wait! Can I go ahead of you guys?"

"Sure!" I was happy that I didn't have to lead, but Goober didn't want to give up his position. Goober refused to take half a step back onto the road, and there we stood, blocking the trail. Goober completely embarrassed me with his stubbornness.

"I'm so sorry!" I said sincerely as Jeremy went around us, half on the hillside.

"It's fine," Jeremy said under his breath. He had racing on his mind and didn't seem to even notice that we were in his way.

With a fresh wind and new horses to ride with, Goober got his motivation back. It must have been the chemistry of Jeremy and his horse, because Goober knew it was race time. The five leading horse-and-rider teams moved out together at a good clip. Goober was doing a nice extended trot and stayed with the competition's horses, who were cantering along to the river. I felt confident in Goober, but riding behind Jeremy intimidated me.

There was no way he would want to be beaten by an 18-year-old girl. My experience was like a drop of rain in the ocean compared to his.

We were coming up to the river crossing, with just enough dusk to light the way.

"How far ahead is the leading horse?" Jeremy asked the volunteers at the site.

"Probably about three minutes," they answered.

I could feel Jeremy's determination; he knew we were within striking distance of the leader. Our group charged through the river. I knew I would get wet feet and didn't even try to keep them dry. Instead, I unhooked my sponge and leaned over Goober's neck, sponging him as we crossed. My dad had told me that Goober loved just standing in the river for a few minutes to cool down, but I didn't have a few minutes, so this was my compromise. Goober liked the cool water, but he was in race mode and stuck close with the group.

As we were emerging from the river, a white horse entered. Almost glowing in the dark, the light-colored horse contrasted beautifully with the black water, its rider hidden in the veil of dusk. Its rider trotted through the river, splashing water everywhere, making ground, and closing the gap on us. Apparently, Heather Reynolds had fixed her boot malfunction because here she was again, joining her husband, Jeremy.

There goes 1st and 2nd place.

I hadn't trained my whole life to be content with 3rd. What if this was my only chance? Goober deserved to have a chance at the win, and so did I. Determined, I decided that I'd hold on as long as we could.

Not long after the river crossing, we came up behind a tired-looking gray horse. This horse and its rider were the only ones standing between our group and the 1st place position.

Goober is way fresher than that horse. I don't have to worry about him coming after the win.

Knowing your competition's race strategy is just as important as knowing the trail and making plans for where to be at what time. Racing against the Reynolds for the last six years, I had an idea of their style. It involved riding slowly at the beginning, picking it up in the canyons, and then tearing it up the last 32 miles from Forest Hill to the finish line.

Holding true, the Reynolds put their horses into a fast gallop. Goober was happy with the change of gait. The three of us soon pulled away and galloped along as dusk turned to dark. Once we were a considerable distance from the others, I tried to keep Goober in a trot as much as possible, but the two other horses were moving about half a mile an hour faster than his extended trot. Goober cantered to narrow the gap between us and the leading horses. He would then fall back into a trot as soon as the distance was closed.

I was holding my breath. I'd never moved out like that after 90 miles. My mind was racing. *What if Goober gets sore from galloping? What if I'm pushing him too hard? I still have another vet check before the finish. Is it better just to slow down and ensure a finish?*

I was determined to stay positive. *If the Reynolds horses can do it, Goober can, too. You can't win if you don't fight. If we lose them now, we won't ever catch them again. They aren't going to ease up at the finish. There is no reason for me not to push for the win and have the most exciting race of my life.*

The conflict within me made me feel sick. I tried to detach from my thoughts and consider things more logically. Goober was in great shape. He would let me know if we should slow down. Winning horses didn't come in looking like they had just been out for a stroll. I visualized some of the previous Tevis winners.

They were sweaty and looked like they had worked hard. I could push Goober a bit harder, and it wouldn't hurt him if he came in tired.

Goober felt good, and I knew I wouldn't have a chance to win if I didn't fight for it. Galloping along the American River, I said a quick prayer that I was making a wise decision; I wanted to ensure that I didn't hurt Goober with my ambition. I had a sense of calmness and felt good about my decision. I could always slow down, but it would be impossible to make up lost time, so I just hung on.

Once I made up my mind, I got full-body chills as it hit me what we were doing. I got emotional for a second, realizing the position that Goober and I were in. I was riding along with some of the best endurance racers in the country, feeling Goober's power and energy under me. I was excited to push him to new limits. We were a team! Only one vet check, the final completion exam, and the Reynolds teams stood between me and the win. My body released a shot of adrenaline. Goober felt it, too, and we were ready to take on the world together.

It was dark by the time we arrived at Lower Quarry. I had a strategy. The first step was to get through the vet check and confirm that we were still in the race, so I could fulfill the rest of my plan. There wasn't one word exchanged as I fast-walked past the Reynolds, snatched a handful of hay for Goober, and went straight to the vet.

A few miles down the trail at No Hands Bridge, my crew was refreshing the webcast as they waited for us. They had a hard time containing their excitement as the results updated, showing that I was among the first three riders in the Lower Quarry vet check. As I made my way to the vet, the crew continued to refresh the browser, hoping that my ride status would stay "on-course" and not transfer to the "pulled" list.

Jeremy and Heather were caught up in their own race and seemed oblivious to the fact that I was even there with them. Here I was, a nobody who had never finished in the top 10 before. I was not a concern for the big-name riders. I overheard snippets of their conversation. They were still concerned about Heather's boot malfunction.

"How's your horse doing?" the vet asked me as he walked around Goober, checking his vitals.

"He's great! We're having a blast, and he feels ready to bring it home to Auburn."

"Can you give me a trot?" the vet asked.

Trotting Goober out under the spotlights of the Lower Quarry vet check recalled a brief memory from my first Tevis—the exhaustion I'd felt six years ago as I trotted Taii Myr out for the vet under the same spotlights. Six years ago, we had kept moving to avoid the cut-off time, and now I kept moving to push for the win.

"Looks good," the vet said. "See you guys in Auburn."

Only six miles to the finish, and then one more vet check to get our completion.

"Let's get this done," I whispered to Goober as he munched on some alfalfa.

I fed Goober an apple at the out-timers before mounting up. I expected Jeremy and Heather to be heading out with us, but Jeremy was still at the vet. I knew I had to put some time between myself and them, so I asked Goober for a fast gallop on the road leaving Lower Quarry.

My crew had a hard time containing their excitement as the webcast updated, showing that I was not only back "on course" to meet them at No Hands Bridge, but had left Lower Quarry two minutes ahead of the 2nd-place horse-and-rider team.

Goober was ready to go home, and cantered willingly. I glanced at my watch. It read 16 miles per hour. *We won't be able to sustain this pace for another five miles.* I felt sick at the thought of having an ever-so-slim opportunity for the win and wasting it in the first mile out of Lower Quarry. I figured Jeremy and Heather would catch us at any minute. That was always their strategy. They "picked up the carnage" on the final few miles of this race, and consistently raced these last six miles very fast.

They probably paced their horses better, and I'll be the person who left Lower Quarry first, just to be passed by two experienced riders with fresher horses. Even worse, what if the riders behind them catch us? There's a whole herd of them, and if they catch up with us, I'll be lucky to finish in the top 10.

I spotted police lights up ahead, flashing blue and red and controlling traffic as Goober and I clip-clopped across the asphalt of the Highway 89 crossing. Suddenly, water rushing under a utility hole stopped Goober in his tracks. He was unsettled and refused to move.

I ran him too hard on the road. I desperately urged him forward. The volunteers were watching. I had to get him across the highway somehow, but Goober's stubborn streak was making it obvious that he had stopped because he wanted to, not because he was too tired. We lost a few precious seconds while he stalled, and I knew the riders behind us were making up ground.

"Are you Heather?" a volunteer asked.

"No, I'm number 203, Sanoma." I replied.

Finally, we made it across the highway and Goober moved out onto the narrow trail. I was having a tough time seeing anything, since the moon hadn't come up yet. I had no idea where the course was, but thankfully Goober knew where we were supposed to be. Riding from glow stick to glow stick, the small artificial lights messed with my eyes and gave just enough light for my pupils to adjust. Still, it always took them an extra second to re-dilate to the blackness, leaving me blind for a few seconds.

It was dead silent except for the sound of Goober picking his way along the trail. I knew spectators were waiting anxiously, and tension was growing as crews for all the top horses were hoping their riders would emerge from the darkness of the trail leading down to No Hands Bridge. My own crew knew from the webcast that the Reynoldses had a hardly mentionable gap, and had discussed among themselves the slim chance that I would be able to maintain the lead.

Emerging from the wooded hillside and making our way down the technical slope to No Hands Bridge, I could sense the suspense up ahead.

"Who is it?" asked the spectators waiting at the historic bridge.

I stayed silent, not knowing what to say.

"Oh my gosh, it's Sanoma!" I heard someone say, but I couldn't identify anyone in the dark. Then my crew stepped forward out of the crowd.

"Woo-woo!" I heard my mom call out. "Go for it, Sanoma! He looks great!" I couldn't make her out, but recognized her voice by its German accent.

I encouraged Goober to pick up the pace, and he fell into a heavy gallop. The spectators at the bridge cheered again. The 2nd-place rider's crew was just as excited as mine. They knew it was extremely likely that their rider would catch me with another four miles to the finish, and had already made a minute on us. Catching up is always easier than running away in front; Goober wanted to slow down to ride with the horse behind us, and the horse behind us was trying to catch Goober.

I turned on the lamp in my GPS watch. "Signal lost," it read. I didn't have a definite answer as to how much farther we had until the finish, and distance can be hard to judge in the dark.

The Reynoldses must be getting close, I thought. We powered up another incline, and then Goober hesitated on one of the switchbacks. In the daylight, I could look into a horse's eyes and see how they were doing, but at night I had to go by feel. Goober's natural laziness made it harder for me to read the fine line between a lack of motivation and fatigue. I let him come to a complete stop and pulled his head over my knee. I quickly turned on my headlamp to look at his eyes, not wanting to leave it on too long so our chaser would know our location. His eye reflected the light as he blinked away the blinding brightness.

"I'm sorry, boy." I felt bad about shining the light into Goober's eye, but his response relieved me. He looked great, and I was confident that I could keep pushing him for the win.

I heard a single set of hoofbeats in the distance. It felt like there was no way Goober and I could hold our lead with still a few more miles to go.

We moved out again, but only at a trot; Goober's enthusiasm to canter was now nonexistent. We crossed a wooden bridge and climbed up more switchbacks. We were about a switchback and a half up the hill when I heard a horse racing across the bridge. I accepted that we would be riding together, and stopped pushing Goober. Unfortunately, Goober was paying attention to the horse behind us and not the trail and tripped over a root that crossed the path. He went down to his nose before catching himself and continuing on.

"Are you okay?" Jeremy's voice came out of the darkness a couple of switchbacks below us.

"Yeah, thanks. Watch out, there's a gnarly root here."

It was mostly silent except for the sound of our horses

picking their way along the technical trail, which required the horses' full concentration due to the narrow path and uneven footing. It was quite the experience, racing through the dark, weaving between trees. At times I thought the course turned left, and Goober made a sudden turn to the right. I soon learned not to trust my eyes, but only my horse. As the trail widened into a double lane, Goober shot up the hill, wanting to leave Jeremy and his horse behind. I let him, since he knew this section of the trail better than I did.

Goober sprinted to the top of the hill, and then he stopped. That wasn't part of the plan. *What is he doing?* Goober was proud that he had won the race to the top of the hill, but the race wasn't over here. We still had about three miles to go. Jeremy, who was right behind us, passed us.

"Is he okay?" Jeremy asked as he passed my stopped horse. He probably hoped I would say no, so he could continue alone.

"Yeah, he's fine, just wants to follow for a bit."

Following was a nice break. Goober was thrilled to be able to coast, and we maintained a good pace.

After following for a while, Goober wanted to take the lead again, but Jeremy's horse, Etta, blocked the trail.

"Can we pass whenever the trail widens a little?" I asked.

"Sure, I'll let you know when it's safe," he replied.

Maybe he's conserving energy, so his horse has some gas left in the tank for the final sprint. I couldn't see how his horse was doing and assumed she was tiring based on her slowing speed. *Or maybe it isn't Etta's decision to ease back.* These thoughts made me even more wary, but I remained prepared to push Goober all the way. This wasn't Jeremy's first time racing for the win, so I had to be prepared for anything—even if Goober seemed stronger to me compared to Etta.

"How about if we pass here?" It looked to me like the trail

had widened, but my eyes had deceived me.

"No!" Jeremy exclaimed. "Stop! Stop! This is not a good place."

I knew that even if the trail wasn't quite wide enough, Goober wouldn't lead us off a cliff and would simply refuse my direction, but I was pleased that Jeremy stopped us from passing at an unsafe spot. My heart raced as I thought of how I had almost misguided us off a narrow trail and down the steep hill. I took a deep breath and patiently waited for a good opening, worried that I would be stuck behind him forever without enough space to pass as the gap to the finish closed with every stride.

Finally, at Jeremy's half-hearted signal, I dug my heels into Goober's accelerator. The second a brief turnout came into view, I took advantage of it to shoot past Jeremy and Etta. It didn't come a moment too soon. Several strides farther, we rounded the bend coming up the final hill to the finish line. I knew that if it came down to a final sprint for the win, Goober would have a good chance; he has a fast kick and hates to lose. I kept urging Goober on, since the last hill is a double lane that would allow Jeremy to pass. Finally, I could see the lights at the finish line.

I locked my eyes on our target and didn't break focus. Horses gain confidence by following your gaze, and mine was straight ahead, fixed on the finish banner. We galloped up the last stretch. Goober knew what I wanted, and he wanted it too. I encouraged him with my words and posture, leaning forward and staring straight ahead. The first horse under the banner wins, and Goober was just as determined as I was to make sure we were the first. The next hundred feet would tell the story.

"Come on, boy, let's bring it home," I whispered to Goober. I could see Jeremy edging up beside me, until Etta and Goober were neck and neck. Suddenly, Goober burst forward with lightning speed to make sure we crossed under the banner ahead of them. As we crossed the finish line, I knew our victory was secure. Goober and I had just won Tevis!

I was in a daze. "Holy cow!" I blurted out, not letting myself believe it. "Thanks, Jeremy, that was the most insane race of my life!"

Jeremy and I embraced as we let our horses drink from the historic trough at Robie Point.

"Who came in first?" asked the volunteer with the clipboard. The crowd watching the close finish knew that I had finished first, but the volunteer hadn't been able to distinguish me from Jeremy in the dark.

"I did," I said in disbelief, almost expecting her to correct me. "My rider number is 203."

"Congratulations!" she beamed.

My legs felt weak under me as my brain processed what Goober and I had just accomplished. A lifetime of training, preparing, and racing had all boiled down to this moment. We had just won the most prestigious and difficult endurance race in the world. I was 18 years old, the youngest woman ever to win—and on a horse acquired from Craigslist!

My head was spinning. I had beaten the U.S.'s top endurance racer, Jeremy Reynolds, in a head-to-head race. It was the closest finish in Tevis history, and after 100 miles through the Sierra Mountains, it came down to about the length of one horse. After being on the trail for 16 hours and 12 minutes, Goober and I were the first ones to cross the finish line out of 184 starters.

I stood next to Goober, not knowing what to do next. My crew hugged me, and it took me a couple of seconds to process what had just happened. They weren't allowed to help out until we did our victory lap in the stadium about a quarter-mile away.

Oh yeah, I still have to get through the final check and untack. I was trying to bring myself back to reality. I sponged Goober a couple of times and fumbled with unhooking his breast collar. Even though I'd taken it off a thousand times, I was having a hard time getting my shaky fingers to unhook the snaps.

Carrying all my tack except my saddle under my arm, I led Goober to the arena for our victory lap. Once we arrived under the stadium's lights, I put Goober's bridle back on, remounted, and trotted him around with Jeremy galloping behind us. We recreated the close finish under the stadium lights for the photographer's camera, and for the stadium sparsely filled with spectators.

A couple of acquaintances came over to offer some help. Reporters for the *Auburn Journal* and various horse magazines stayed at a safe distance while we worked to get Goober ready for his final vet examination.

More than anything, I wanted the peace of mind of our completion. I wasted no time getting to the vet, knowing Goober might not have the best cardio recovery. At least he wouldn't have time to stiffen up.

Trotting back to the vet, he gave me two thumbs up. Before he even told me, I knew Goober had earned his completion.

"Congratulations!" the head vet said, hugging me. "You are a Tevis champion!"

I was on cloud nine and couldn't stop smiling. Despite my paranoia all day, Goober didn't feel sore once, and not one vet had mentioned it or noticed any irregularity in his gait.

"Can I get a picture?" a photographer asked.

I was sure I was quite a sight, with dark electrolytes highlighting my blonde braids and trail dust glued to my face. I had helmet hair and black grime all over, where the dirt had stuck to my sweat. Goober had dirt on his nose from when he'd tripped. But, despite our appearance, our happy smiles and glowing pride said it all.

Once we had the vet's official completion, a few reporters flocked around for interviews. I answered the question "Where did you get your horse?" and immediately saw the spark in the reporters' eyes at the headline this would make.

> **"Sanoma Blakeley and RA Ares Bay Win 2019 Tevis Cup**
> The 18-year-old, riding an Arabian gelding found for free in a Craigslist ad, edged out three-time winner Jeremy Reynolds in a race to the finish."
>
> —Marsha Hayes, *The Horse*

A couple of hours after our finish, Goober was happily munching on some alfalfa, under his cozy blanket on the dimly lit side of the stadium. I had entrusted him to our crew as my mom and I made our way to the finish line to wait for my dad to arrive. Another rider at Forest Hill had asked Pa to sponsor her, and when she finished with a different sponsor, we knew something had gone wrong.

"Congrats on finishing, Caroline!" Mom said. "Do you know where Wasch is?"

"He pulled back," she replied. "Wasch's horse was a little sore on the foot where he lost the boot. So he said he was going to walk the last six miles on foot."

About an hour later, my dad walked under the finish banner with Luke in tow. Sure enough, Luke looked a little sore. Walking with him from the finish line to the stadium, we brought Pa up to speed.

"Who won?" he asked, not knowing the news yet.

"Guess!" my mom said, but based on her excitement, it wasn't too hard for my dad to figure it out.

"Sanoma?" he answered incredulously.

"Yep!" I said, almost hopping with excitement as I walked next to him. "Can you believe it? It was a crazy race against Jeremy."

"Oh, man! At Quarry, they told me that the two competitors came in together, but I didn't know who won. They thought maybe Sanoma had, but weren't sure. It must have been a heck of a last six miles. I saw tack along the trail—looked like maybe Jeremy was dropping stuff to lighten the load."

"Oh really! That's crazy, but it doesn't surprise me."

Unfortunately, my dad and Luke got pulled at the finish line. Riding 100 miles and not getting the credit for it stings. We tried to relieve Luke's pain by replacing his boot, but what he needed was rest and time, which we didn't have. Once a horse crosses the finish line, they only have 40 minutes to show to the vet. Finish line pulls are the worst, but in our hearts, Luke had finished. He ran the whole 100 miles, and that is something to be proud of. Heather Reynolds had also been pulled at the final finish line exam for the boot that was causing trouble.

Barrak had pulled Quicksan at Francisco's. She was having an off day, and never seemed to settle into race mode.

My dad was disappointed with his race's outcome but so happy that Goober and I had won. He couldn't have been prouder. We were the winning family at Tevis!

The atmosphere at the finish line was exhilarating and captivating, unlike anything I'd ever experienced. It was a huge party. Riders, crews, and horses scattered throughout the fairgrounds all sympathized and celebrated with each other, knowing what everybody had just gone through. Throughout the night, the announcer's microphone interrupted at intervals to announce new arrivals at the finish line, followed by cheering as horses and riders came out of the dark to reach their goal.

At around four o'clock in the morning, the adrenaline finally wore off, and I got some much-needed rest. My cheeks hurt from smiling by the time I went to bed. The second my head touched the pillow, my eyes closed, and I got a few hours of happy, restful sleep. While I was sleeping, the Auburn, California, fairgrounds welcomed dawn, along with the trailer that arrived carrying Quicksan and Barrak.

CHAPTER 14

The Aftermath

The train whistle brought me out of a deep, dreamless sleep. We had finished, but the race still wasn't over. At 10:00 AM, the top 10 horses would present for a drug test and show for the Haggin Cup, which is the award given to the horse finishing in superior condition. It is similar to the Best Condition award given at local rides, but has more politics involved. It doesn't take factors like weight and time into consideration, but does include horsemanship.

I was content with my win, knowing it was doubtful that Goober and I would double-cup and win both the Tevis and the Haggin. Many riders would rather win the Haggin Cup, and thus race more conservatively in order to have a fresher horse at the end and be a contender for this award. I had ridden to win Tevis, and hadn't tried to conserve Goober for the Haggin. Winning the actual race was more important to me. For me, it was clear and straightforward: the first horse across the finish line wins. There was no way to deny that and no room for interpretation.

A couple of hours before the presentation, my crew and I iced our horses' legs. After icing and bandaging Goober, I hopped on him bareback and was immediately reminded of how chafed and sore I was. I rode him around camp to loosen him up. It was surprising how relaxed his muscles were after running 100 miles the day before.

A few riders recognized me and Goober. "Congratulations!" they said as we rode by.

My seat bones were sore, but before long, Goober and I had loosened up enough to get into a smooth rhythm. He felt terrific. Maybe we did have a chance at winning the Haggin Cup.

Now it just came down to the final presentation.

"Should we bring Quicksan along for company, or take Goober alone?"

This was a big decision. Goober was very attached to Quicksan. If she stayed at the trailer, Goober would be upset that she wasn't with him and make a scene. On the other hand, if she was with him, he might be complacent and not look as fresh. We decided he should go alone.

In the stadium, waiting in line for the vet to draw Goober's blood for the drug test, we had a little time to reconsider our decision. Goober was neighing loudly and being unruly. True, he didn't look like he had just completed a 100-mile trek across the Sierra Mountains, but he was also making me look like I had no horsemanship skills. The other nine horses in the arena were standing quietly. Every once in a while, one would respond to Goober as he threw his tantrum.

"Shut up, Goober!" I growled. "I'm going to go deaf. Just be quiet." As much as I loved him, this was getting to be a little much. He was embarrassing us, swinging into everybody and throwing his head and pawing to let us know just how ticked off he was.

Pulling on his halter halfway through a whinny got his attention, and he went quiet. It only lasted a couple of minutes, and then, like a kid who didn't get their way, he went off again.

"Our first-place finisher is Sanoma Blakeley and RA Ares Bey." The announcer was calling us into the stadium's center, where the vets had gathered under a blue pop-up tent to do a thorough examination for the prestigious award.

"You better behave," I told Goober sternly, leading him into the lion's den.

The first vet walked over to us and explained how the exam would go. I was instructed to trot Goober out in a straight line about 250 feet away from the vets for the Cardio Recovery Index (CRI) test. One vet would measure his heart rate before the trot out. We would then run out and back and, a minute after we returned, the vet would re-measure Goober's heart rate. The difference in the numbers would give the highly trained vets a good idea of how recovered he was.

I knew Goober's excitement wouldn't help him keep a low heart rate. Showing no respect for the vet, Goober bumped into him with his shoulders. There are few things vets dislike more than a disrespectful horse. So, even though Goober was full of energy and looked like the most recovered horse in the stadium, we would probably lose significant points because of his obnoxious behavior and elevated heart rate.

With Goober at my shoulder on a leadline, we ran straight toward the cheering spectators in the stands. I remembered the day 12 years earlier when I'd been sitting in those same stands and had resolved to be standing where I was today, in the center of the arena with the winning horse.

Following the CRI evaluation, the lameness specialist examined Goober's legs, palpating for swelling and soreness.

"Please follow the chalk marking and run straight out," the vet instructed. "Then run in a circle, following the chalk to the right, and then run the circle to the left. It doesn't matter which way you run first." His instructions wouldn't have made much sense had I not seen it done over the last several years.

After our two circles, I was pleased with how Goober looked. Sure, he could have done better, but it was still a pretty decent showing. The rest of the evaluation was painless, besides Goober misbehaving. In my heart, I knew that we wouldn't win the award because he had been so unruly and, from a vet's standpoint, didn't present perfectly.

I was surprised when the announcer called out the 3rd-place horse next. The Reynolds always showed their horses for the Haggin Cup, and they had chosen not to show Etta. She must have been sore. The fact that Goober had beaten her and looked so great the next day brought a smile to my face.

Monk, ridden by Lindsay Fisher, was showing. Although he'd come in 9th place, Monk was a legend. He was 17 years old, and this was his fifth Tevis finish in the top 10. Everybody loved Monk. On his CRI trot out, the crowd exploded.

"Well, there's your Haggin Cup winner," my dad said.

Happy with my Tevis Cup win, we headed back to the trailer to put Goober away, pack up camp, and get ready for the award presentation and lunch at noon.

The award presentation seemed to take forever. The staticky, unclear microphone and chatter of the crowd made the acknowledgments preceding the ceremony next to impossible to understand. Then the race manager started calling up the 98 actual finishers to receive their certificates. Only 53 percent of the riders at Tevis had actually completed it this year. The top 10 finishers received their awards and made brief remarks.

As the 10th-place rider paraded her horse under the pavilion, Goober settled down a little. Despite all the years we'd dreamed of giving the winning speech and all the joking about what we would say, I still had no idea what I was going to say when they handed me the microphone in a few minutes.

They announced us, and then handed me my buckle and other awards. "Would you like to say a few words about your horse and your ride?" the ride manager asked.

Not really, I thought. But Chuck, the ride manager, wasn't asking; he told me politely that it was my turn to talk.

"We had an incredible ride yesterday." Goober whinnied in agreement as my voice echoed through the pavilion. "I couldn't have asked for a better way for it to end. Goober was an awesome horse all day. He's just an awesome horse." This brought a chuckle from the crowd. Obviously, I thought my horse was awesome.

"Goober knows he's special, too," I continued. "He is a bit cocky, and he is quite the character. He is definitely a lot of work, but . . . well, he's my dad's horse." Goober pushed me with his shoulder as the crowd laughed at my modest sentiments about the horse who had won Tevis.

"Do you have anything to say to your dad?" Chuck asked me.

"He is the most amazing dad in the world. I am so thankful that he let me ride Goober. Yeah, and I couldn't have done it without my dad, my horse, or my family."

I felt myself getting choked up from the nerves combined with having just achieved my lifelong dream. I decided to cut my speech short before I got too emotional. Now that the time had finally arrived, I couldn't think of much to say.

When we got back to the trailer, I took off Goober's award ribbons and packed them up along with all of our other stuff. Although he hadn't won the Haggin Cup, I was still enormously proud of him.

We gave the horses a quick, cool bath before loading them

in the trailer for the long haul home. On the way, our phone was constantly notifying us of new messages.

I didn't realize just how big of a deal winning Tevis was until I got messages from people I didn't even know congratulating me. I received calls and requests to be interviewed for TV, radio, podcasts, and horse magazines. The local *Gold Country Media* headlines read:

By a Horse's Length
Fantastic finish gives 18-year-old her first win at 2019 Tevis Cup

A few days after Tevis, one of my good friends who lives in Bend asked me to join her for a walk. She trains mustangs, and even though we don't ride together often, we are great friends. Walking up Lava Butte together to watch the August sunset, I was still a little sore from Tevis when I got a call from a news reporter from CNN. I retold the Tevis story for the interviewer as I climbed up through the manzanitas, half out of breath.

A week after Tevis, we were having a lazy day at home when the phone rang—a California number. Unless we had just won Tevis or had a horse for sale, we usually didn't answer out-of-state numbers.

"Guess who just called?" I asked my family.

"No idea," my mom said. "Probably Tevis-related."

"It was a film producer from Los Angeles. He wants to make a movie based on our Tevis win!"

"You totally have to go for it," my brother said.

A week ago, I wouldn't have even dreamt I would be getting a call to be the subject of a movie, but now it could be a possibility.

"I don't know, that seems kinda scary," I said. "You know how many cheesy horse movies there are on Netflix. Besides, what if they make me out to be someone I'm not?"

"You can worry about that later," Barrak said encouragingly.

"You know how many girls would love to have a movie made about them?"

We joked about famous actors playing the roles of different individuals in the family. Maybe it didn't sound so bad after all.

I also started receiving sponsorship opportunities, and people offered to give me their horses. When I typed my name into a Google search, results started popping up. It felt odd and exciting to be noticed and recognized as the youngest woman ever to win the Tevis Cup.

Goober was cockier than usual. He knew he was hot stuff, and continued to push everybody around. He was definitely happy to be back in the pasture with Quicksan and all his pals, enjoying his well-deserved vacation from riding.

I was satisfied that I'd accomplished my goal, but now I had to set a new one. When people asked what my next aspiration was, I didn't want to put pressure on myself, so I answered, "I might try Tevis again, but I'll probably just focus on finishing." If Goober finished Tevis one more time, he would win the Robie Cup, an award presented to horses that finished Tevis five times. But on second thought, I wanted to hold our title and win two years in a row. I decided I'd have to ask Goober, but I felt sure he'd be up for defending his title, too.

CHAPTER 15

A Fork in the Road

After a life-changing moment like racing for the win at Tevis under the dark California sky, there was nothing that could have further strengthened the bond between me and Goober. I'd always had a soft spot in my heart for him, but now my heart was just mush for my special boy. I loved that horse, and I'm pretty sure the feeling was mutual.

After a few well-deserved months off, we were back to training. Goober and I were ready to defend our title in 2020. By March, we had a strong team of four horses that would be pretty unstoppable if everything continued smoothly.

However, nothing ever goes as planned. COVID-19 stopped the race season completely. Things we had taken for granted before, like horse races and getting together with friends, were not allowed. We figured it would be all settled down within a few weeks, but it wound up affecting plans for the whole year. Training throughout the winter and riding in the freezing temperatures and the dark was all for nothing when they canceled Tevis. So, I eased up on Goober's training and enjoyed some slower-paced rides through the spring and early summer.

Things settled down a little as the season progressed, and a couple of smaller races were still held. They followed the COVID-19 requirements, such as social distancing and wearing masks. We picked up training again for the Bighorn 100 endurance event. Some considered it to be as tough as Tevis, but I'd never gone because of the long drive to Wyoming and the timing conflict with Tevis.

I replaced Tevis with Bighorn in my calendar and charged ahead with training for this bucket-list ride. Even though there were still a few things to look forward to in the summer of 2020, it was generally a restricted year. We didn't know how long the pandemic would last, and I had other goals that I wanted to achieve in my life. I wanted to travel and maybe try some of the other world-famous endurance races—the Fauresmith in South Africa, for example, or the Tom Quilty Gold Cup in Australia.

Money was always tight, and the pandemic brought further financial uncertainties to our family. So when Heather Reynolds contacted us, representing a client looking for a top-quality horse, we discussed selling our personal horses. Unfortunately, we only had three horses that Heather's client was interested in: Goober, Pyro, and Quicksan. I cried at the thought of selling any of the three, but losing Quicksan would hurt the least, so we offered to sell her. They acknowledged our offer on Quicksan but then asked for a price on Goober instead. Despite my tears and our insistence that he wasn't for sale, they persisted, determined to own a Tevis winner.

"I don't want to hold you back," I said, "especially if I'm not even in the country in a couple of years. But I love him and I don't want to say goodbye." I knew that, ultimately, it was my parents' choice.

"This may be our only opportunity to sell Goober for a good price," my dad remarked. "He is already 11 years old, and we don't know what the future will hold. With Tevis and pretty much the whole race season canceled, it could be the perfect time." It seemed like a reasonable argument.

"If we sold Goober, we could take some of the money and

upgrade the horse trailer," I said. "That thing has been all over with us and is looking pretty rough. I'm almost embarrassed to hang my sponsor's banners on it, with all the rust and dents."

"That would be nice," Mom added. "We've had it for over 14 years, and it was used before that. Maybe we could even upgrade the truck a little. The paint is chipping pretty good, and it would be kind of nice to have something that was made in this century."

"Or, if we were to upgrade the truck, maybe we could even get a four-door so Barrak's knees aren't in his chin on long drives," I joked.

"Why don't we send them a ridiculous price?" my mom suggested. "Even if they accept it, there's a good chance he won't pass the vet exam. Then we'll have no regrets about not trying to sell him and can enjoy keeping him."

After some negotiating, Heather's client decided that Goober was too expensive, so we agreed to show them Quicksan.

"So, who's your client and what's he looking for?" my dad asked Heather. After her long flight from Florida, we'd just enjoyed lunch together and were catching up on racing stories.

"Mike is from Turkey," Heather replied. "He got a grant from the Turkish government to start an endurance team representing his country for the World Championships. He hired me and Jeremy to be his coaches and buy some of the U.S.'s best horses to make up the Turkish team. His team is in Florida, and he hopes to qualify for the 2022 World Championships in Italy. So, if he bought one of your horses, we would try to qualify them for the championships."

"That is so awesome!" I said. "How cool would it be to have one of our horses race in the World Championships?" I imagined

Quicksan on an airplane, flying to race with some of the best horses in the world.

We introduced Heather to our herd and took her for a ride to give her a feel for the animals she was interested in buying. Keeping our options open, we let her ride Goober before having her switch to Quicksan. We set business aside for a while to enjoy the ride and share more horse stories and small talk.

"So, what do you think?" my dad asked the following morning. "Would your client be interested in Quicksan?"

"To be honest, I don't think they would be a good match," Heather replied. She knew her client's desires, needs, and riding ability.

"Would he still be interested in Goober if the price were lower?" my dad asked.

"Absolutely," Heather said. "Mike would love Goober. He is the perfect horse for him."

I smiled. I loved the thought of my special boy racing at the next level of competition and showing the world just how good he was.

"Could Sanoma be a groom and accompany him to Italy if he went?" Pa asked, always wanting to include something more than money in the negotiation.

"Yes. And if you ever want to ride Goober or visit him in Florida, you are always welcome. Mike said that if you guys want him back once he retires, you can have him."

I couldn't offer Goober the same opportunities that the Reynoldses and their client could. They would take Goober to the next level of international competition; I preferred racing locally with my family. The higher levels of the sport were more cut-throat and sometimes political, so it didn't appeal to me. Although it would feel like someone had ripped my heart out, I knew it was what was best for him—my feisty, competitive, darling Goober.

Not even a few minutes after we accepted Mike's contingent offer, he called my mom on the phone. He thanked us for selling Goober to him, and offered for us to come visit him anytime in Florida. He said that if Goober ever needed a vacation, he could even come back to Oregon for a brief stay.

Mike was sincerely excited to own a Tevis winner and promised to take good care of him for us. In addition to Heather's promise, he also told us personally that we could have him back when he was done racing.

I accepted the bittersweet reality that if Goober passed the vet exam, he would be heading to a new home in Florida. Ironically, a vet from Bend Equine, the vet clinic that had initially diagnosed Goober with OCD as a yearling, came out to do a thorough exam of the now-Tevis winner.

The vet performed extensive flexion tests and radiographs, and he reported just how tough Goober was. His OCD was still there, and the results of the exam were less than perfect. But it was not nearly as big of a concern as the last potential buyers had made it out to be. It certainly was not what had caused his soreness before Tevis.

The vet exam results didn't make Goober any less desirable to Mike, but he used this opportunity to renegotiate the price. The lower offer gave us a second chance to get out of the negotiation. We rejected the offer and were perfectly content with keeping Goober.

However, after several weeks of reflecting on whether we'd made the right call, we had some serious reasons to reconsider. The pandemic wasn't getting much better, despite our optimism that things would be "back to normal" by the summer. Being restricted and unable to travel made me yearn for a life of adventure beyond the saddle. Seeing pictures of endurance races in other countries helped me realize what I really wanted to do for the next few years of my life: travel.

So, despite all of the emotions and everything we had been through together, the best, most logical decision was to let Goober continue his career as a racehorse and go places I wouldn't be able to take him, and at the same time allow myself the financial freedom to pursue my own goals. We accepted the offer.

Goober was the fourth horse I cried about letting go, and I cried more about him than all the others combined. I knew it wouldn't be easy, and waiting a little over a week for the shipper to pick him up only made it worse. When I fed the other horses, Goober would come to me begging for treats. He had no idea that within a few days, he would be in a trailer heading east. His ignorance of the situation dug the knife deeper into my heart.

I knew that once he was gone, it would be really painful to be reminded of him, but also that I would want something significant to remember him by. I had pictures of me and Goober at races over the years, but I wanted more to remind me of the kind of horse he was—not just a racehorse, but my friend. I'd seen some beautiful photos of girls with their horses and wanted to do something like that with Goober. Except, instead of horses with flowing manes, it would be my racehorse with his sport-cut mane, rippling muscles, and veins popping from his shiny coat.

"Do you think I could do a photo shoot with Goober?" I asked my mom.

"That's a great idea," she said. "But we'd better get on it, since he's going to be picked up in the next few days."

My family had never done a photo shoot before. We were very practical and had always taken our own pictures. We had a lot of friends who were photographers, but horses are challenging to photograph because they are always wiggling and moving, and I wanted someone professional who I would be relaxed and natural around.

"How about Dave?" my dad suggested. Dave Brownell was a good friend of ours who had moved to the Oregon coast. We had a few of his magnificent photos hanging on our walls. Dave could make something as ordinary as ice skating on a pond look like a real piece of art. He had taken action shots worldwide for *Outside* magazine, and every new photo was more impressive than the one before.

So, Dave drove out to capture the bond between me and Goober through his lens. Goober hated having his forehead petted, but he yielded enough to let me rest my forehead on his. With my eyes closed, I forgot about the camera and shared a few brief seconds with Goober. Heads together, we were one in that moment. I inhaled and came to peace with letting him go.

Even though Goober is now missing from the pasture, our relationship is printed for posterity and hangs on my bedroom wall.

The shippers wanted to get an early start on heading south to California before their long journey across the States. It was going to be a beautiful late-July day, and it was hot despite the early hour. I loved those days in the summer, with the dew-covered grass, cooing of doves, and cloudless blue skies. I'd already said goodbye to Goober multiple times over the past few days. Our horses had come and gone over the years, but Goober was always the constant. He was the first to welcome the horses after a ride, and always waited at the gate for us when we went to the corral.

Goober whinnied at me as I walked down the driveway. He was expecting me to bring a treat or maybe a bucket of grain to lick out, but I just had his halter in my hands and a couple of carrots in my pockets. The reality of his departure was undeniable as I put his halter on for the last time.

I handed the lead rope to the shipper, and Goober loaded into the trailer without hesitation, trusting that we would always be there for him. Once the trailer door closed, he started pawing, confused as to why his friends weren't coming and why he wasn't in our trailer. That's when I lost it; all of my preparation for this moment didn't matter anymore. My best friend was leaving, and I felt like I had let him down. His nervous whinnies echoed in the foreign trailer, and I couldn't stop the tears that were streaming down my face.

Even though I knew this was for the best, I couldn't think logically. Horses move on faster than humans do, and I knew that in a few weeks, Goober wouldn't even remember what he'd had in Oregon. As long as he had food, friends, and a job, he would be happy. But, of course, a part of me wanted him to miss me.

I offered him a carrot through the trailer window.

"Goodbye, boy," I said, biting my lip through the tears. "I'm gonna miss you."

The shipper noticed my anguish and came over to hug me. I hated showing my emotions, especially in front of people, but the shipper understood what I was going through. "I'm so sorry you have to say goodbye to your buddy," she said. "We'll take great care of him on the trip. We have shipped a lot of horses for the Reynoldses, and he'll have a good home."

Then, finally, they were ready to hit the road.

"Goodbye, Goobs," I said through the closed horse trailer window.

Goober threw a tantrum as the trailer headed down the driveway. Even though I hated his tantrums, that was Goober, and that was what made him who he was. After nine years of growing up together and everything we had been through, the heartache was unbearable. This goodbye was the hardest of them all.

The next day, we were on the road ourselves. This would be one of the first out-of-state races without Goober in the trailer in the last several years. Wyoming-bound, my brother had graciously lent me Quicksan to race at the Bighorn 100.

After two days on the road and some of the most gorgeous countryside I'd ever seen, we received an email from Dave Brownell with the pictures he'd taken of me and Goober. I posted some of my favorites on my Instagram account. Trying to think of a caption, I settled on:

> Fun photo shoot with my favorite boy before saying goodbye. Gonna miss you, Goober. 📷 Make us proud as you continue racing and going to places we couldn't have taken you 🐎 🐎 We had quite the ride together 🖤

Driving through the desolate landscape between Montana and Wyoming, I scrolled through those photos. Goober was the most powerful racehorse I'd ever had the privilege of riding, but he was also a horse who trusted me as much as I trusted him. And I trusted that we would see each other again.

As the road forks and Goober and I take our different paths, we will see where our journeys lead us. Hopefully, our paths will cross in Italy, when I am crewing for him at the World Championships. The adventures are just beginning. Until we meet again, my friend.

Team "Rescue Goober"

I had Goober's race record bookmarked on my phone, and for a few days after each of his races, I refreshed the webpages to witness yet another victory by our special boy.

I'd kept up with Goober ever since we'd sold him, and our paths had even crossed a couple of times at races. It was nice to be able to see him and tell him that I missed him, but seeing him owned by someone else was painful for my still tender heart. He had continued to win races on the East Coast and, for a while, he was doing very well with his new endurance team. He made us proud.

However, the flame of racing soon began to die, and it seemed that Mike's endurance team was slowly fading. It appeared that he'd set his sights too high; he had bought five of the best horses in the United States, but endurance isn't a sport you can buy your way to the top of. His endurance team had done well under Jeremy and Heather Reynolds' coaching, but it seemed that competing in the world championships was unrealistic. Within two years, the Reynoldses were no longer coaching Mike's endurance team, and his race record wasn't reporting any additional races.

As our horses' coats started to grow longer late into 2022, I received a text message from Haley: "Hey! Mike is having his horses repossessed. Karen has Goober if your family wants to reach out to her about getting him back."

Mike had sent his five endurance horses, including Goober, to a trainer in Texas, who was supposed to rehab him from a surgery after he had sustained an injury.

Haley had included the trainer's number. I called her without delay, and she told me that Mike hadn't paid her for several months of training. According to their contract, she could claim the horses for non-payment, and she was in the process of legally repossessing all of Mike's endurance horses. I insisted that my family wanted Goober back when she was legally ready to rehome him.

As the days grew shorter and the leaves began to cover the pasture, we consulted some reputable endurance riders who were more familiar with the situation. They claimed that Goober and Mike's other four horses were in rough shape. Rumor had it that these horses had been neglected and were skinny. It had been several months since I'd seen a photo of Goober, but the description of these five horses made me sick. I wasn't sure who was responsible for the neglect. It seemed that everyone was pointing fingers, but one thing was for sure: these top athletes desperately needed to get out of the situation they were in.

We were still apprehensive about the legal aspect. We didn't want to put our entire horse budget for the next year into buying Goober and paying for shipping to Oregon, and then have things backfire on us and not legally own Goober. Mike had the kind of money and legal team that made us double-think any kind of legal battle.

While doing our due diligence, my dad's Google search presented an interesting result. The headline of an Organized Crime and Corruption Reporting Project article read:

Notorious Money Launderer's
Lavish Life and New Business in Miami

The photo at the top of the article showed Mike, riding one of the horses that the trainer in Texas was repossessing.

My heart raced as I read through the article. There was no denying that this was the same man who had bought Goober. There were references about his involvement in endurance racing, and his fancy stable in Florida that Goober was registered under.

The article called him "The Turkish Gatsby." Apparently, he had faced a 130-year prison sentence before accepting a plea deal. In just five years, it was said, his network had moved around $20 billion.

This type of lifestyle and aliases were things I had only seen on television. But here was a man I had not only personally met, but also entrusted with my dearest friend, Goober.

As the first snow dusted the barn, I was packing my bags for an overseas adventure. I was heading off to spend some time with my family in Germany, and then a friend was going to join me to explore some other gems of Europe. While double-checking my flight itinerary for the following day, I quickly scrolled through our stable's social media. One particular post froze my thumb and made me sit up straight. Along with a photo of a neglected horse that looked to be in bad shape, the post warned about the woman who had been training the horse. It was bashing her reputation and saying a lot of negative things about her and the way she took care of the horses in her care. The post was about the same woman who was rehabbing Goober.

I immediately called her up. There was no need for pleasantries; she knew why I was calling. I tried to convince her to let me inspect Goober personally; I had a couple days' layover in Texas to visit friends on my way to Europe, and the timing couldn't have been better. Despite my insistence, she declined my offer and instead sent me some photos of Goober. Even in those pictures, I could tell that he didn't have the same spark in his eye as when my family had owned him.

We were determined to get Goober back. We weren't sure who or what to believe. Regrets wouldn't accomplish anything, so instead we made a plan of how to get him back and make sure that he never had to face something like this again. We did everything we could to ensure that when the time came, we would be ready to bring Goober home.

As difficult as it was, we had to be patient while we waited for the legal developments. As soon as the lawyer confirmed they were ready to move forward with rehoming the horses, the trainer contacted us to make us aware that she had to sell Goober, Etta, and three of Mike's other horses through a public auction that would take place at her stable. There were a lot of rumors— that she was stealing the horses, that it wasn't legal, and so on. But the one that worried me the most was that she had a lot of other people interested in buying Goober. Those people would have the chance to purchase not only a proven 100-mile endurance horse, but a Tevis winner!

I stayed up all night watching the comments as people asked for additional information on the horses that were going to be at the auction. My only comfort was that, with only a week until the auction, people might not invest without first meeting the horse or having a veterinarian perform a pre-purchase examination. My parents desperately wanted to get Goober back, too, and I knew they would do just about anything to ensure his safety.

My parents arrived in Dallas a little after midnight on Monday morning, several hours before the auction. Traveling on only an hour of sleep, my parents and the Payne girls sent me a photo of them driving down a dark Texas interstate. The photo caption read: "Team 'Rescue Goober' on its way."

I could hardly concentrate on anything else. I was in Vienna at the time of the auction and, despite being in one of the most beautiful cities in Europe, I longed to be with my parents and good friends to know of the situation with Goober.

I bugged them again 45 minutes before the auction was scheduled to start: "Have you made it?"

"Yes, dealing with the lawyer," was my dad's brief reply.

I bombarded them with questions, but the only reply was a GIF my mom sent of a duck drumming, with a caption that read "drumroll please." A little while later, she sent pictures of two horses that were being auctioned. Neither of them was Goober. I recognized one of them as Etta, the horse Goober and I had raced against at Tevis in 2019. The other horse was from the photo in the OCCRP article.

My mom was not answering any of my questions or requests for more information. I desperately wanted to be there and to know what was going on. After waiting months for the legal developments to come to this point, I couldn't stand another second of not knowing what was going on. The old wood floor of my Airbnb groaned as I paced around the room, refreshing my messages every few seconds.

Finally, my notification bar lit up. A few seconds later, I felt the walls closing in on me. We had done so much to ensure that Goober would be ours again. We had been so close. I re-read the heart-sinking text. My eyes went a little blurry as I stared at the two words: "Goober sold."

I sent a million more messages, requesting an explanation of what was happening. I knew my parents were in the middle of the auction and couldn't pick up my calls or respond to my messages, but I felt left in the dark. They would let me know all the details as soon as they had a minute, but I didn't want to wait for an explanation.

I continued pacing. I opened the fridge, but I didn't have an appetite. I closed it again and told my good friend my speculation of the situation. I expressed my slim hope that Goober had sold to my parents, but I didn't want to allow myself to hope for that.

Several long minutes later, I received another text from my dad. I fumbled to pick up my phone and open the photo. The picture contained three smiling Payne girls, my mom, and Goober.

"He is now ours," was my mom's brief message.

I couldn't believe my eyes. I dialed their number but knew they were in the middle of a transaction and wasn't surprised when they didn't answer. Mom's text was enough to allow me to breathe out the lungful of air I had been holding in for the last few months. I slumped on the couch, leaning my head against its back, and let my chest rise and collapse dramatically a couple of times as I processed the emotions that were flooding through my body.

I re-read the message from my mom before relating the news to my friend. Hearing myself say, "Goober is safe," made it feel so definite.

Regan sent me a short video clip of Goober being auctioned off, and my parents raising their hand and saying they would buy him. Seeing my beautiful parents stand up for Goober almost brought me to tears. Goober had gone from being a free horse we had gotten on Craigslist to the most expensive horse we'd ever bought by almost triple. It didn't matter; he was worth every penny. He had given so much for us, and we owed it to him.

I couldn't contain my excitement that Goober was ours

again. I hardly let myself envision this dream, and I kept waiting for myself to wake up, or for Mike to say we had stolen his horse. Instead, I got to see a photo of my parents escorting him off the property.

Goober was coming home. My heart was bursting with happiness, and I couldn't wait to greet him with open arms when he got off the transport at his final destination: Blakeley Endurance Stables in central Oregon.

Everything went quicker than I expected, and I was still out of the country when Goober arrived back home. I woke up in the middle of the night to check my messages, and my heart sang as the light of my phone screen illuminated my dark room, revealing the photos my mom had sent. I was ecstatic to see the two Tevis winners, Goober and Pyro, in the same picture. It was a perfect start to the new year.

My parents sent me updates over the next few days, including a photo of Pa riding Goober. As much as I was enjoying my trip on the other side of the Atlantic, my heart was torn. I wanted to be home. I wanted to be with my parents and my Goober.

"How is Goober doing?" I asked my mom on just about every phone call. "Is he happy to be home?"

"Yes! He is so happy to be home. Although I forgot how much of a goober he is." Ma was happy to report that Goober and Pyro had picked up their friendship right where they left off. I considered cutting my trip short, just because I missed my family and horses, but they were the constant that I could always come home to.

As I embraced my parents at the Redmond Airport, I felt home. Seeing the sun tuck in behind the familiar Cascade Mountains and walking arm in arm between my parents, my only worry was that I would have to wait another 20 minutes to greet Goober.

He was standing in his favorite spot, right where he had been almost two and a half years earlier when I had said goodbye to him. With his head over the gate, greeting me, I broke into a jog. I ran down the driveway and hopped over the fence.

Goober hadn't changed much. I threw my arms around his neck and embraced my friend, our chests together. I hugged him for a couple of seconds before taking a step back. Then I grabbed a handful of his mane and swung myself onto his back.

He didn't have a halter on, but I draped my fingers around his neck. I locked my hands together in front of his chest and buried my face into his grown-out mane.

"It's good to see you again, Goobs," I whispered with flushed cheeks.

Goober's ears flickered towards me as he wrapped his neck around one of my arms and nuzzled my leg. His eyes sparkled, and the memories of racing Tevis together flooded back into my mind. There wasn't a worry in the world that could take me out of that moment.

I reached over and clasped his muzzle in my hands. I gave him a gentle kiss on his velvet muzzle. My heart felt the exact opposite of the times that it had let go and said goodbye.

Despite the ups and downs, the highs and lows, the victories and heartbreaks of owning and racing horses, this reunion gave me peace. The bright moon peeked out from behind a snowy Gray Butte as I ran my fingers through Goober's fuzzy coat. I couldn't help but let a single tear roll down my cheek as I let out a long, satisfied sigh. Goober and I were home.

Afterword

Over the years, I've won races, gotten pulled, and said good-byes as horses went to new homes or drew their last breaths. In the end, though, this isn't just a sport or a hobby—it's a way of life, a passion. I love racing horses, always striving to improve and help them reach their limits. I didn't win Tevis because I got lucky; Goober and I fought for every inch of it. It took a lifetime of racing, trial and error, late-night analyzing, walking off hills where I couldn't feel my toes because of the cold, riding 20 miles with a broken arm, checking on my horses in the middle of the night, and so much more. But there is nothing in the world I would trade it for.

In the end, life isn't about what people think. It's about having a family that sticks by my side. It's about having a horse that brings me to tears because of the pride I feel about the partnership we created. The trust that can't be bought, that has to be built.

It isn't the victories that count. For me, it's holding onto my memories and continually chasing my dreams. It's the pain of saying goodbye and closing a chapter, knowing there is a new one waiting to be written, but having no idea where it will lead. That's what makes me feel alive.

Photo Credits

Courtesy of Teviscup.org and the Western States Trail Foundation: 6

Courtesy of Teviscup.org: 124

Author's Personal Collection: i (all), ii (all), iii (all), iv (bottom), v (all), vi, vii (all), ix (bottom), x (top), xi (top), xii (bottom), xiii (top), xx (bottom), xxiv (all)

April Depuy: iv (top)

Monica Bretherton: viii (top)

Pekka: viii (bottom)

Tevis Webcast Volunteer: ix (top), xii (top), xiii (bottom), xv (top)

Steve Bradley: x (bottom)

Dominique Cognee/kumbadigital.com: xi (bottom), xix

Erin Glassman: xiv (top)

Tevis Webcast Volunteer Crissy Tadlock: xiv (bottom), xx (top)

Michael Kirby: xv (bottom), xviii

Rob Osborn: xvi, xvii

David Brownell: xxi, xxii (all), xxiii (all)